**THE EPIC TALE OF THREE
INCREDIBLE COAST TO COAST WALKS
BY HER NINTH BIRTHDAY!**

RACHAEL

A Remarkable
Record Breaker

Rachael aged seven at the start of her epic adventure.

THE EPIC TALE OF THREE
INCREDIBLE COAST TO COAST WALKS
BY HER NINTH BIRTHDAY!

RACHAEL

A Remarkable
Record Breaker

JOYCE BUXTON

Rachael: A Remarkable Record Breaker
Joyce Buxton

First published in 2013 by Buxton and Moseley.
Old Water View Patterdale Penrith Cumbria CA11 0NW

Front cover: The summit of Place Fell is just off the C2C path but they could see
Old Water View from the top so Rachael just had to do the extra climb!
Back cover: Catching the wind at Carlton Bank.

This book is a work of non-fiction based on the life, experiences and recollections of
Ian and Rachael Moseley. In some limited cases the names of people, places, dates and
sequences or the detail of events have been changed solely to protect the privacy of others.
The author has stated to the publishers that, except in such minor respects not affecting
the substantial accuracy of the work, the contents of the book are true.

A CIP catalogue record for this book is available from the British Library.
ISBN: 978-1-909461-06-2

Printed and bound in Great Britain.

Contents

Wow Daddy, these are beautiful!

Preface

This is the story of my 'granddaughter'[1] Rachael Moseley who celebrated her ninth birthday at Robin Hood's Bay on April 17th 2013.

It is an account of a wonderfully brave and inspirational little girl who completed the first of her three Coast to Coast Walks from St. Bees to Robin Hood's Bay aged seven years and completed her third crossing on her ninth birthday – 3 x 192 mile walks in less than two years makes her a remarkable record breaker!

As readers can imagine, we are all incredibly proud of this amazing little girl, not just for her achievements but for the way she completed this massive triple challenge. She absolutely enjoys walking with her equally amazing dad, Ian – she is so full of joy and wonderment and is utterly alive and in tune with her surroundings. Whatever the weather or terrain, she sees magic in everything around her – the glory of butterflies, flowers, trees, cloud shapes, shadows in the landscape, sunshine and sparkling water – she marvels in every colour, sight and sound – she is an absolutely incomparable companion – a true, true walker!

---

(1) Some years ago, Catherine, Rachael and their Daddy, Ian Moseley adopted me as 'Grandma Joyce' – (it is an honour that I treasure).

Dedication

This book is dedicated to The Patterdale Mountain Rescue Team for the wonderfully brave, prompt and unpaid service they willingly provide to all in difficulties on the mountains, fells and surrounding countryside. They constantly risk their lives to save others.

What is the
Coast to Coast Walk?

For readers who are unfamiliar with the C2C and those who are planning to walk it for the first time, the Coast to Coast Walk is a long distance walk – around 192 miles – across England from one coast to another as originally designed by Alfred Wainwright. (Indeed you can still buy a copy of his book and his two maps.)

It has a definite beginning, usually St. Bees in Cumbria and an ending at Robin Hood's Bay in Yorkshire. Traditionally at the start you dip your boots in the Irish Sea and pick up a pebble from the beach. You carry this pebble across the breadth of England and throw it into the North Sea where you dip your boots again. You can, of course, walk it in reverse starting at Robin Hood's Bay.

Although the traditional route passes through fabulous and varied scenery and is generally waymarked, as Wainwright always pointed out, the route taken is up to the individual – there are no specific rules! However, many people especially those walking the C2C for the first time, faithfully follow Wainwright's route. It gives them confidence. More adventurous walkers plan their own route. The choice is yours! Just make sure that you can read a map and use a compass efficiently – relying solely on a GPS or Sat-Nav may not be a good idea!

As you will read, Rachael's Route mainly follows the traditional one but necessarily at times, Ian chose a different route according to the weather and the condition of the terrain. Safety was paramount – especially as his daughter Rachael was only seven years old on her first C2C and only eight years old when she started her third C2C!

She celebrated her ninth birthday at Robin Hood's Bay at the end of her C2C3.

The Beginning – the 'birth' of a wonderful walker

It all started in 2007 when Rachael was around three years old. She was sitting with her Daddy, Ian, by Goldrill Beck in the lovely garden of her home, Old Water View, Patterdale – a well known hotel and restaurant owned and run by Ian. Some guests, as they frequently do, asked Ian about the direction of the C2C path from Patterdale to Shap. As always Ian pointed out the path up the side of Place Fell towards the Hause from their garden and explained,

'You just cross the bridge over Goldrill Beck then follow that path up to the Hause, turn to the right and you'll soon reach lovely Angle Tarn, then up to The Knott, over Kidsty Pike and down to Haweswater. Then it's just a gentle walk up to Shap. You'll love it!'

Rachael was listening intently and studying where Ian's hand was pointing. 'Daddy, what's on the other side of that mountain?' She asked.

It was a beautiful day and all of Ian's guests had departed so he put Rachael in his backpack and carried her up to the summit of Place Fell. She ran about, laughing and clapping her hands in happiness and was absolutely fascinated when Ian pointed out the 'dolls' house like' image of Old Water View and Patterdale village far below.

'It's magic, Daddy! 'She cried, 'I don't need a carry. Can I walk down, please?'

Bless her – she managed to walk about a third of the way down before Ian put her in his back pack again. She was so happy; she sang and chatted all the way back home. From that moment, Rachael's love of walking and her enthusiasm and ambition to be a Coast to Coaster began – a wonderful walker was born.

When she was aged five she began to ask questions about the Coast to Coast – quite understandable as most C2C'rs stay at Old Water View including the famous Alfred Wainwright and more lately Julia Bradbury visited.

She asked... 'Daddy – is the Coast to Coast, that van which brings the bags to our house and takes them away next day?'

She was, of course, referring to the Packhorse and Sherpa vans which transfer walkers' luggage along the C2C.

Ian explained that the C2C was a very long walk right across England – you started at St. Bees, got your feet wet in the sea and picked up a pebble. Then you carried that pebble nearly 200 miles all the way to Robin Hood's Bay so you could throw it into the sea and get your feet wet again.

You know what is coming next!

Training at Buttermere with an ice cream.

'Wow!' shouted Rachael, 'Can I do it. Please Daddy! Please! Please! Can I do it with you, please?'

(Ian, of course, has walked the C2C many times and led walking parties.)

'Yes, darling, we can', promised Ian, 'but you will have to wait until you are 15. It is such a long walk and very hard in places.'

The discussion ended there but Rachael did not forget because about a year later when Ian and she were out on the fells and had just climbed Sheffield Pike, Rachael suddenly said quite 'out of the blue':

'Daddy, you know that I **could** do the C2C **now**, don't you?'

Initially Ian replied that she was too young but then secretly thought to himself:

'It's amazing but she's right – she is such a fantastic little walker and a wonderful companion – we could do it together using my unique C2C knowledge and a good safety back-up plan!'

And so the idea of the first C2C was born. Obviously because of Rachael's age, a great deal of planning had to be done including allowing a slightly longer time than most adult Coast to Coasters aim for. A target of 17 days was set. Also Ian, naturally concerned for Rachael's safety, arranged support vehicles all the way.

Neither of them could wait to start in the summer of 2011.

Rachael's first
Coast to Coast – 2011

From St. Bees to Kirkby Stephen
via Ennerdale, Rosthwaite, Grasmere and Patterdale

The first part of the C2C was done by using Old Water View as a base – walking each day to the next stop and returning home to Old Water View each evening. However they did stay overnight at our favourite hostel – Black Sail Hut in Ennerdale.

The start was not auspicious!

They set off by bus and called in at Keswick on their way to St. Bees because Ian wanted to buy Rachael a new waterproof jacket. Somehow they managed to lose each other for 20 minutes in Booths Supermarket! (Incidentally, Ian teaches navigation!) Whoops! Luckily they found each other and somewhat shamefaced, especially Ian, they eventually reached St. Bees.

The weather the first morning was glorious – bright sunshine and a gentle breeze. Rachael was incredibly excited as she duly picked up two pebbles – one for herself and one for her sister, Catherine. Then after the obligatory dip of her boots in the Irish Sea, she set off at a run up the beach and cliffs towards the lighthouse. Ian had a job to keep up with her!

From here they set off inland facing east towards Robin Hood's Bay some 190 miles away! An awesome challenge for a little seven year old girl! Blissfully unaware of this and just completely happy to be walking with Daddy, Rachael could hardly wait to reach their target in two days' time when they would be at Black Sail Hut in the wild but lovely Ennerdale Valley.

She had heard so much about this wonderful remote Bothy set in magnificent scenery from her Daddy and me. We just knew that this would be Rachael's special place and we were right!

About half way up the very long path in Ennerdale, Rachael was desperate for a wee. Ian suggested that she just popped behind a nearby bush as no-one was around – no-one except an inquisitive sheep who watched her intently.

'I think that sheep liked my pink knickers – cheeky thing!' giggled Rachael, 'Perhaps it's never seen pink knickers before' and she skipped on happily.

She was absolutely captivated when she finally reached Black Sail Hut and so full of joy and happiness that she ran around jumping, skipping and singing with arms outstretched just like Maria in 'The Sound of Music' – she was ecstatic!

Left: Rachael aged seven at the start of her epic adventure. **Right:** Dipping her boots in The Irish Sea.

The stunning cliff top path on St. Bees Head.

Beautiful Ennerdale Water in the rain.

Ian watched her from the hut, bouncing along in the evening sunshine, with tears of pride and joy in his eyes!

After Black Sail, Rachael and Ian continued their C2C journey via Grasmere and up to Grisedale Tarn. It was a beautiful day – bright sunshine again and a clear blue sky. As usual Rachael was dashing ahead of Ian leaping like a mountain goat up the steep, rocky path on the right-hand side of the beck. When the tarn unexpectedly appeared she just stood there open-mouthed, completely entranced!

'Wow, Daddy,' she exclaimed in wonderment, 'Look at this amazing tarn – isn't it fantastic!'

As walkers who have descended the valley towards Patterdale from Grisedale Tarn will know very well, the wind suddenly began to blow very hard and Rachael had to shelter behind Daddy holding onto his rucksack most of the way down because it was blowing her off her feet!

Where the path is more level and runs above the stream, there is a wood and incredibly Rachael spotted and identified a tawny owl! She is so observant – Ian had walked straight past it.

Around 4pm, as she was running rapidly ahead, inevitably she missed her footing on the stony path and fell quite heavily injuring her knee. Did she cry? Of course not! A quick clean–up from Daddy and she soldiered on, limping but still happy towards home at Old Water View.

From here they walked via Bampton Grange to Orton where there is a quite a famous little Chocolate Factory. Rachael treated herself to a thoroughly deserved chocolate mobile phone before they returned home.

Left: Dancing in cold water with bare feet at Black Sail. **Right:** Grisedale Tarn in perfect sunshine.
30 minutes later they could hardly stand up in the strong winds.

Left: Just loving the sunshine! **Right:** I did not believe my dad when he told me there was a chocolate
factory on the C2C ... YUMMY!

Left: Posing as we close in on Kirkby Stephen. (note that Rachael was map reading on this part of the trail).
Right: Serious walker during the day but still a little seven year old playing in the pub sandpit.

Old Water View was becoming too remote to use as a base so they continued their amazing, magical C2C journey staying at a variety of B&Bs and hotels on the way.

I delivered their luggage to Old Croft House, Kirkby Stephen having dropped them off back at Orton from where they planned to walk through to Kirkby Stephen. From here, completely free-of-charge, The Packhorse Company would transport their heavy luggage every day as far as Robin Hood's Bay.

On the approach to the town, they had to cross a huge field full of cows, horses and sheep. Unfortunately the farmer suddenly appeared on a noisy quad-bike panicking all the animals! They scattered everywhere and for a while it was quite scary! Rachael sensibly managed to dash to safety in a sheep tunnel within a stone wall and Daddy was saved by the farmer's young son who herded the animals to the other side of the field. Undeterred, Rachael marched merrily on until they reached their destination and was delighted to be greeted by a flock of red and green parrots! Magic!

She had a fit of giggles when she spotted a toilet abandoned in the middle of a garden (obviously as a result of renovation work.) Laughingly she said to Ian: 'It must be very windy and cold using that Daddy – I hope ours isn't like that!' It wasn't!

That evening this extraordinary little girl who had coped so maturely with every adverse condition so far on her C2C walk was happily playing like a very small child building sandcastles in the pub sandpit. A little girl just having fun!

She phoned me that evening full of news and utterly elated and eager to continue her great adventure with Daddy.

The second part of Rachael's first Coast to Coast – 2011

Kirkby Stephen via Keld to Richmond and on to Danby Whiske

Unfortunately next morning as they left for Keld, the rain just poured down and very low clouds were scudding across the dull grey sky. In these conditions, Nine Standards Rigg, a high, exposed boggy moorland ridge, can be very dangerous with deep, soggy peat – just one quagmire after another and in such poor visibility even experienced walkers can have great difficulty in locating the vague path. Knowing this and obviously concerned for Rachael's safety, Ian decided that the road route was the most sensible option.

Rachael, always curious, was intrigued by a loud, croaking sort of sound very close to them.

'What's that funny noise, Daddy?' she enquired.

Ian explained that it was a grouse and right on cue several appeared just ahead of them in the heather.

'Daddy, Daddy!' begged Rachael, 'Can I catch one, please?'

'Of course, you can, darling,' replied Ian, knowing full well that it was impossible, 'Good Luck! If you can catch one, you can keep it!'

Undeterred Rachael kept trying different methods, all unsuccessful, at intervals all the way into Keld in fact all she managed to catch was a single discarded feather which she proudly put in her daypack and still has it to this day.

These attempts at capture were interspersed by Rachael measuring herself against every tall foxglove that she spotted on the verges. Sadly most of them were far taller than Rachael but eventually, to her joy, she found one that was slightly smaller and thought that one with its beautiful pink 'trumpet-shaped' flowers, was by far the best! Her antics kept both of them amused and the miles sped by.

They both kept hearing sounds of shooting and Ian had to explain that this was what game hunters did – they shot the grouse for a sport! Rachael was genuinely incensed by this and thought it very unjust so at the end of the day, they both agreed that they were going to 'adopt a grouse' – and from that day onwards, it would be their favourite bird!

Left: Tall foxgloves – little walker! **Right:** The beautiful River Swale just outside Keld.

In one place, the mist was so thick that Ian could scarcely see the road ahead. He turned round to check on Rachael, who for once was behind him and discovered her standing completely still staring upwards, utterly mesmerised,

'What kind of bird is that Daddy?' she whispered, 'It's not moving.'

Ian peered upwards too and eventually could make out the vague outline of a kestrel hovering silently above them.

'It's a kestrel, darling,' he answered marvelling at her acute sight – how had she seen it!

'Wow! 'Said Rachael awed, 'I wish I could just float in the air like that.'

She loved sitting quietly by several of the wonderful water falls of the River Swale – she was completely entranced – gazing at the sparkling water tumbling down, marvelling at the spray ' shining like diamonds' and listening, as she said to Ian 'to the music of the water.' She truly does have the gift of seeing magic in everything.

Shortly after they had crossed the border into Yorkshire, they overtook two young men who were also doing the C2C and had stopped for a picnic. Determined not to let a mere girl and a small one at that beat them, they packed up quickly and sprinted past Rachael disappearing into the distance. This episode was repeated later, when they stopped to eat their lunch not realising just how near to Keld they actually were. So as they rounded a bend, Rachael and Ian were surprised to see these two young men again, one of whom had obviously stopped 'to answer a call of nature'. Ever the opportunist,

Left: Planking! **Right:** Half-Way and the watershed – the rivers flow east from this point.

Rachael took full advantage of this pause and sprinted ahead to Keld Lodge where she triumphantly touched the wall there exclaiming,

'I've beaten them, Daddy! Hurray!'

'You only got here first because we were ill and had to stop!' grumbled one of the youths.

'What a shame!' Rachael smiled triumphantly, understanding completely that they were telling lies because they did not want to admit that she had beaten them, 'Sorry, no excuses – I really did get here first!'

What a competitor!

That evening as they ate their meal, a man who was sitting at a nearby table got up and confronted Rachael and Ian as well,

'Excuse me but are you trying to convince people that this little girl has walked all the way from St. Bees, I don't believe it – she must have had a carry!'

He rudely turned round and walked away so Ian had no chance to reply and Rachael just ignored him. Revenge is sweet though because in a few days' time, this man was to get his comeuppance!

Later that evening Ian explained to Rachael that Keld was where the C2C and the first ever long distance walk, the Pennine Way crossed each other. As expected, Rachael's response was,

'Really, Daddy, can we walk that one too, please!'

The remains of Swaledale's mining heritage.

Keld via Reeth to Richmond

Two memorable ladies enlivened the walk into Reeth the following day. The first was an American lady who was walking the C2C the same time as Rachael and Ian. She always seemed to set off before them but Rachael and Ian frequently overtook her yet amazingly she kept 'popping up' in front of them again. As there were several helicopters flying that day, Rachael decided that the American lady was somehow getting a lift and christened her 'The Helicopter Lady.' They solved the mystery later on.

The second lady was me – Grandma Joyce. Every stream that Rachael saw on the way from Keld to Reeth, she asked if that was the one that Grandma Joyce had fallen into three times and got a crinkly bottom!

(On my first C2C on the moors' route into Reeth I slipped on some mossy stones trying to cross a stream in Cringley Bottom – not once but three times – twice desperately trying to climb out – as I sat in the very cold water I christened the stream 'Crinkly Bottom' for obvious reasons. This had really amused Rachael!) Not exactly knowing the location, Ian eventually just chose a stream. Needless to say, Rachael did not fall into it – sensible girl!

In view of the competitive remarks and disbelief of the previous evening, Ian decided to have a bit of fun with Rachael. He picked her up and carried her all of 12 inches and put her down again.

'Now, Rachael,' he said smiling down at her, 'you haven't walked all the way after all!'

'Oh, yes I have!' shouted Rachael and promptly walked back to the spot where she had been picked up and very deliberately walked forward again, 'I've walked this bit twice!'

You just cannot beat that little girl – she was absolutely determined to walk every step and nothing and no-one was going to stop her!

Rachael and Alan (the support and back-up man) outside Springfield House, Reeth.

Reeth onwards

When they reached the pub in Reeth, they met Ian's friend, Alan who was to be their support driver for the next few days. Rachael gave him a big hug – she was one happy, happy girl!

Later as they were sitting outside on The Buck Hotel patio enjoying a well-earned drink, Rachael still full of energy and bounce asked Ian if she could go and play on the village green just opposite them.

'Yes, of course you can, darling, 'answered Ian, 'But be careful; remember you are wearing your crocs!'

Rachael had changed from her boots to her pink crocs to give her feet a deserved rest. 'Crocs' – for readers who are unfamiliar with this type of footwear, are like rubber open backed sandals and sometimes, like 'flip-flops', are difficult to keep on your feet on uneven ground or when you are running.)

They were just marveling at Rachael's antics – she was absolutely 'full of beans' – laughing and singing, skipping, jumping and running in sheer joy when there was a terrifying scream and a sickening bone-crunching sound – SPLAT!

Everyone shuddered and looked up in horror. Disaster! Rachael had tried to hurdle the low retaining wall that is around the green but had caught the front of both of her crocs on the top. She was pitched violently down onto the hard, unforgiving concrete below, headfirst! Ian and Alan truly thought that she would have some horrifying head injuries and that this was going to be the end of Rachael's C2C.

Ian sprang up and rushed to pick her up dreading what he would find. She clung to him, sobbing with pain and in shock.

Miraculously when he cleaned her up and examined her, Ian was amazed to discover that although she had quite a few nasty grazes and would obviously be bruised next day that was the extent of her injuries!

Left: Cartwheeling the C2C – as you do! **Right:** Posing between Marske and Richmond.

As soon as Rachael realised that she wasn't too badly hurt, she bravely stopped crying, wiped her tears and in a tearful voice, admitted to Ian,

'Oh, Daddy, I was so scared that I wouldn't be able to carry on walking with you. That's why I was heartbroken and cried so much but I'm okay now and we can carry on tomorrow, can't we?'

'Of course, we can,' responded Ian amazed at her courage and determination, 'but you are going to be very sore in the morning.'

'I don't care!' said Rachael emphatically, 'I'm going to finish this C2C – you see!'

Ian looked at her with pride – he had absolutely no doubt that his wonderful little daughter would do just that!

Rachael's next goal was the historic town of Richmond and the day was absolutely baking hot – really too hot to be able to walk comfortably. For once Ian underestimated the amount of water they would need and they ran out long before Richmond. However Alan, their support driver, came to the rescue with several bottles of welcome cold water! He certainly earned his 'Brownie points' that day!

Just before Richmond, when they were crossing a large beautiful lush green field, Rachael, eyes sparkling, suddenly asked, 'Daddy, please can I do cartwheels on this lovely grass, please?'

Ian replied that it was very hot and she really ought to conserve her strength but Rachael was determined,

'I'll be okay, Daddy – just watch me!'

And off she went – doing awesome cartwheels across the whole length of the field corner to corner – at least 200 yards – grazes and bruises completely

Left: The plaque here says that behind Rachael is Wainwright's favourite view of Richmond... mmm, lawn mower required! **Right:** Cheers! It is always great to have a coke at the end of the day's walk.

forgotten! Ian watched her in admiration – 'Where does she get all that vitality, especially after her accident yesterday?', he wondered.

Then she noticed some white strangely shaped clouds gathering overhead and spent quite some time trying to decide which animal they looked like – eventually she decided that they were most like an elephant. She is just so interested in everything around her, she inspires you to see the world anew through her eyes and you are often challenged to answer her questions – like the name of a mysterious butterfly resting on a plant near the wall of the field – a black one with red spots – even Ian didn't know that one so he had to look it up later (it was a six spotted Burnet moth).

Rachael is a wonderful companion and she certainly 'keeps you on your toes'!

On reaching Richmond, they had to do some necessary shopping for Daddy. Before they started, Ian was so engrossed in ensuring that he packed everything he thought that Rachael would need plus some spares, he completely forgot to pack enough shirts for himself. He only had one shirt and one spare and as Rachael pointed out, he was going to be very smelly soon so new shirts were essential!

'You are a silly, funny Daddy forgetting your shirts!' She giggled, wrinkling her nose as she helped him to choose,

'I do love you!' and she gave him a huge hug.

Then they solved the helicopter lady mystery – Rachael spotted her getting out of a taxi!

'Wow! That is cheating!' She protested and triumphantly added 'I am going to walk all the way!'

Tall corn – little walker.

Danby Whiske to Ingleby Cross

It was another very hot day as they set off for Danby Whiske. When they reached Bolton-on-Swale, Rachael was fascinated to see a table at the side of the road full of essentials for hungry and thirsty C2Coasters – drinks, energy and chocolate bars, fruit and crisps with an Honesty Box for payments. Actually they thought this was such a good idea that they decided to adopt it and now, outside Old Water View, there is a large box containing similar key necessities and an Honesty Box too. It is well used and all the money is given to the Patterdale Mountain Rescue Team!

Thankfully, when they reached the pub at Danby Whiske it was open and they were made very welcome. (Years before, as readers will know, Wainwright had complained that it was always shut when he passed.)

Rachael treated herself to a large Aero bar and a cup of hot chocolate – a double chocolate hit! This remarkable seven year old had certainly earned it – many times over!

The next day started quite dramatically in two very different ways!

First incident was when they had to cross the fields of a farmer who, obviously, did not like C2Coasters!

To deter walkers, he had fastened a plastic rat and a skull on the stile just where you had to put your hands to pull yourself over. His plan failed miserably because Rachael thought that it was a huge joke and deliberately posed on the

Left: Yummy! That is 122 miles done and just 70 to go. **Right:** You Dirty Rat!

Left: Do I really have to cross? **Right:** Playing with Pip, Jet and Leader.

The Chain Lady at Ingleby Cross.

stile for several photos. Then she decided to try and catch some of his chickens – they were of a similar disposition to their owner and looked at her in a supercilious way and just flew off! Fortunately the farmer did not see her!

The second incident was a just beyond the farmer's fields where there is a train line which you have to cross. Rachael looked horrified!

'You aren't supposed to cross railway lines, Daddy!' she protested. Rachael had been thoroughly schooled about the danger of railways.

Ian explained that on this occasion, it was quite safe to cross as it was on the official C2C path and you could see clearly in both directions and hear too. Rachael was not convinced so Ian crossed the line and after looking very carefully, he beckoned her over. Looking unusually apprehensive, Rachael crossed the line very gingerly. Unfortunately Ian's photo of her just did not come out properly so she had to go back and do it all again! She was not impressed!

Outside the Blue Bell Inn at Ingleby Cross, Rachael was fascinated by a very unusual sculpture of a woman made completely from chains. Of course this was a good excuse for lots of posing and photos. She is very photogenic and loves having her photo taken.

That evening they were invited for dinner by some friends, Ruth and Gerry who had stayed with Ian at Old Water View. Rachael had an absolute ball in the garden frolicking with their three Labradors Pip, Jet and Leader who was old and blind. Rachael hugged him especially tenderly. Then Gerry took her to his allotment part of the garden where she was able to choose her own vegetables for the evening meal. Magic! (Rachael and Ian are both vegetarians so this was a special treat.)

They all had a fabulous relaxed evening with a wonderful dinner in the garden in beautiful sunshine – a perfect end to a dramatic day!

To Chop Gate, the Lion Inn and Fryup Head

The next part of their amazing walk was along the Cleveland Way over Carlton Bank on a partially paved track. As often happens on this stretch, the clouds were low so it was rather misty and drizzling quite hard. However the mist kept drifting and swirling and at times it lifted briefly to give entrancing glimpses of wonderful views below. Rachael thought this was awesome – just like a series of photos of different scenes, each equally magical. She 'was walking on air!'

They stopped for a drink and snack at the unusual Lord's Stone Café – a really welcoming place that is built into the bank so that at a distance just looks like a huge green mound. Here they met their friends, Trish and Kevin who took over driving the support vehicle from Alan. Rachael loves Trish – she is the only lady who can brush Rachael's hair and put it in a French plait

Daddy told me there was a sofa on top of the mountain hidden in the clouds and I thought it was another of his many Dad tricks.

without any complaints from Rachael!

Their climb up the steep path to the panoramic viewpoint of Cringle End was in hazy sunshine but the sun shone brightly on them as they climbed up again to the high and spectacular Wainstones. As always Rachael posed for photos on every interesting rock formation and there are many, and in front of every breath-taking view. However the session was cut short by a sudden cloudburst – the rain absolutely poured down – it was torrential and the lightning really scary for Ian being concerned about his beloved seven year old. However Rachael thought it was great. Enthusiastically she scrambled down over the rocks and down the now squelchy path completely oblivious of the fact that she was soaked and her boots, like Daddy's, were full of water! Did she complain? Of course not! She loved it!

They were picked up at Clay Bank Top by Trish and Kevin and taken down to their overnight stay at Forge House run by a lovely couple who have a smallholding. Rachael was thrilled to be able to sit on their cow – she really does have an affinity with animals of all kinds.

That evening they all went to the local pub where they met again that disgruntled and unbelieving man from Keld Lodge.

'Bet you didn't walk today, Rachael, he crowed, 'not in all that dreadful rain and lightning!'

Rachael smiled and just borrowed Ian's camera,

'Oh yes I did!' she exclaimed smugly, 'Look at our photos – they prove that I walked over the Wainstones with Daddy and he will tell you I climbed down

Left: The Wainstones... **Right:** They should be called the wet stones!

in all that dreadful rain!'

Shamefaced the man retreated – 'his tail between his legs'. (Told you he would get his comeuppance.) Shortly afterwards, his wife came over to Rachael and Ian and apologised.

'We really didn't believe you. Sorry!' she said 'Can we give you a donation for Mountain Rescue, please?'

She offered £5 which Rachael and Ian accepted graciously – another triumph!

Trish drove the support vehicle next day so that Kevin could walk with Rachael and Ian. It was an uneventful day as the path is a flat cinder track that once was the Ironstone Railway going past Bloworth Junction to the famous Lion Inn at Blakey Ridge. The only memorable incident was an embarrassing one for Kevin. The path is wide – over moorland – with no trees and very few reasonably sized bushes. Kevin waited until Rachael was some distance ahead before he dashed behind a small bush to wee. At that moment Rachael turned round and laughed merrily,

'We know what you're doing!' she chanted – Kevin had a very red face.

They reached Blakey Ridge early as this section is only about seven miles long, so after chatting to Trish, they agreed to walk on to the strangely named Fryup Dale where Trish would pick them up.

Of course she arrived before them and fell asleep in the car. With a mischievous grin Rachael crept up to the car and poor Trish was rudely awakened with a loud BOOO! Bless her she still drove them back to the Lion Inn – what a lovely lady!

The Cleveland Hills with a glimpse of the North Sea.

Left: Bloworth Junction, North York Moors. **Right:** Hanging on!

A hug from Fat Betty.

Left: Heather moors – North Sea far on the horizon. **Right:** Hiding in the amazing heather at Fryup Dale.

Fryup Dale Head to Grosmont

Kevin volunteered to drive the support vehicle next morning so Trish could walk with Rachael and Ian. He dropped them off at the head of Fryup Dale where they had finished yesterday, very near to the aptly named huge, white boundary stone – Fat Betty. (She must have been a lady of generous proportions!)

The track here over the heather moor is wide and gravelly but the excellent easy walking is enhanced by the wide-reaching views of Eskdale and the Matterhorn-like peak of Roseberry Topping some ten miles distant to the north. Rachael skipped happily ahead in the sunshine as they walked down to

Left: Beggar's Bridge, Glaisdale. **Right:** Grosmont Station is the start of the final day's walk.

We love Glaisdale.

Glaisdale and over the much photographed 17th century Beggars Bridge – another chance for Rachael to pose for the obligatory photo!

Beggar's Bridge, (171 miles of the C2C) was the target for the day but as they were all full of walking, they decided to carry to Egton Bridge and through the welcoming shade of Arncliffe Wood to Grosmont – home of the fantastically restored station of The North York Railway.

Now they were faced by the endless steep climb out of Grosmont – this hill (one in three and over a mile long) puts a sinking feeling into the stomachs of many C2C walkers whether it is tackled at the end of a day or the beginning of the next one. Did it deter our intrepid walkers? Of course not! Rachael and

Trish marched up steadily hand in hand, singing 'The Grand Old Duke of York' right to the top where the road curves to the right and stopped at the cattle grid before the open moor. Here they had reached the marker of 177 miles of the C2C – only 15 miles to go for our brilliant little walker, Rachael!

Kevin picked them up and took them back to their B&B in Glaisdale and then they all went to the local pub for a pizza and chips. While they were waiting and enjoying a well-earned drink, pizzas were served to some diners on a nearby table – they were enormous! Concerned that the size would outface Rachael, Ian said,

'Just look at the size of those pizzas – you really don't have to try to eat all of yours, Rachael, it is quite alright to leave some – just eat as much as you can, darling.'

He need not have worried; Rachael demolished all of her pizza and chips and ate Daddy's chips too! They all looked at her with astonishment, admiration and disbelief! Where did she put all that food?

The final day – Destination Robin Hood's Bay!

Beautiful sunshine greeted them for their final day. Magic! This would be Rachael and Ian's longest day of the whole C2C – 15 miles! Trish walked with them again down to the picturesque Littlebeck where the shallow sparkling stream is the home of some very noisy ducks.

They crossed the road and followed the woodland path gently upwards to a massive boulder out of which, amazingly, a remarkable shelter with seats has been carved. In beautiful lettering outside, is inscribed, 'The Hermitage – 1790' with the initials GC. More posing and memorable photos!

From here they followed the trail to the spectacular Falling Foss waterfall.

Rachael, however, was more interested in her reward of a big ice-cream from the tranquil tearooms just beyond Falling Foss. As they were sitting down enjoying their well-deserved treat, Rachael noticed a man going past them. He was around 30 years old and, obviously, a fellow C2Coaster. That was NOT to be allowed! Rachael sprang up and rapidly followed him with Ian and Trish trailing behind. At the entrance to the strangely named Bottoms Lane, they overtook the unfortunate man who had stopped to have a sandwich.

'Hello, again!' said Rachael in a friendly way – but ever the competitor, she whispered to Ian,

'He is NOT going to beat me to Robin Hood's Bay – no way!'

Kevin joined them just beyond High Hawsker where, together, they followed the picturesque cliff path to their destination. The views out to sea are absolutely stunning but for once Rachael didn't really look. She was completely

Left: The Hermitage. **Right:** Falling Foss Waterfall.

He-he! — (well!! Bottom's up!!).

One mile to go on the cliff top path above Robin Hood's Bay.

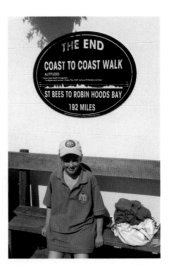

Left: Looking down at RHB for the first time. **Right:** I did it!! (One C2C down, two to go! – except Daddy doesn't know that – yet!)

engrossed in watching that man, ensuring that he was some distance behind them and couldn't overtake.

When Robin Hood's Bay came into view for the very first time, Ian pointed out the beach just over a mile away and said to Rachael,

'See that beach down there – that is the beach at Robin Hood's Bay. You have been walking towards that beach all the way from the beach at St. Bees – 192 miles – isn't that awesome!'

Rachael was quiet for a while and looked very thoughtful and a little sad.

'I don't want to stop, Daddy! Can we go home for two days and see mummy and then can we do this all over again!' she pleaded.

'No! Darling,' responded Ian firmly, 'once you have done the Coast to Coast that's it – you've done it. There are lots more challenges in the world.'

''That's not fair!' Rachael cried downhearted and sat down on a nearby rock, 'I'm tired.'

The very first time she had ever said this – as readers will realise, she wasn't really tired just upset.

'That's okay, darling,' replied Ian sympathetically, 'just have a little rest, a drink and a chocolate bar and you'll be fine.'

Then Rachael spotted her adversary – the man! He was catching them up! Tiredness completely forgotten, Rachael sprang up and set off with renewed vigour along the grassy path towards her goal. She actually ran down the hill towards the beach at Robin Hood's Bay, with Ian, Trish and Kevin in hot pursuit!

Alan joined them. He had walked along the beach from Whitby so he could greet this marvellous little walker and congratulate her.

The picture says it all – an amazing Daddy and Daughter moment.

Rachael ran onto the beach – the tide was right in.

'I've done it! Hurray! 'She exclaimed and added, 'and I've beaten him!' – And so she had as that man, her competitor, appeared a few minutes later.

She was absolutely ecstatic – exploding with excitement and sheer triumph!

She threw her pebble and the one she had carried 192 miles for her sister, Catherine, into the sea and then, of course jumped into the sea herself and tried very hard to pull Daddy in too.

She was incandescent with joy – she just glowed!

Ian watched proudly, trying hard but unsuccessfully to hold back his tears, what an incredible achievement for his amazing little daughter and importantly not one single blister!

Rachael was seven years, three months and 23 days when she finished her first C2C! What a star!

They duly went into Wainwright's Bar to sign the register and have a celebratory drink and then visited The Plaque Shop at the bottom of the hill to order a special plaque for Rachael.

The owner was full of admiration – he told them that Rachael was the youngest person for whom he had ever made a plaque and it was a real honour to make one for her.

On the way home, Rachael again pleaded with Ian,

'Are you really sure, Daddy, that we can't do it again. I really, really want to!'

'No!' replied Ian emphatically, 'you will definitely not be doing the C2C again – there are too many other fun things we can do together!'

Read on and you will find out who won!

Money raised by Rachael

On her first C2C, Rachael was sponsored by innumerable people – guests at Old Water View, family, friends and neighbours, passers-by etc. – few of them had really expected her to complete that astonishing challenge for a seven year old but were full of admiration and very happy to sponsor such an inspirational little girl.

Actually she raised £1000 for her school in Patterdale and £350 for Patterdale Mountain Rescue Team – a wonderful achievement.

Coast to Coast 2 – 2012

How it came about

Just a week or so later, after Rachael had completed her wonderful Coast to Coast Walk, around 11 pm. Catherine came downstairs in tears. She gave Ian a big hug and said sadly,

'Daddy, I feel really jealous of Rachael. Everyone is talking about her doing the C2C and saying how marvellous and brave she is. I do wish that I had done the walk with you when you asked me!'

She paused a moment, hugged Ian again and then asked,

'Daddy, if you were to change your mind and decided to do the C2C again, could I walk with you?'

'Yes, you can if you really want to,' replied Ian, 'but you'll have to do some serious training. If you are prepared to do that, then I'll book the C2C again.'

Catherine then become a little fearful,

'Daddy, I think I've changed my mind – I'd love to do it but I really don't think I can!'

Ian responded quickly, 'Oh yes! You can, Catherine, you absolutely can do it and you will!'

At this point, Rachael, who had followed her sister downstairs and was listening hidden round the corner in the kitchen, burst into the lounge and protested loudly,

'That's not fair! I kept asking you to do the C2C with me again and you kept saying NO!'

What could Ian do – he really had no choice!

'Okay, you two, we'll do the C2C again but this time as a family' – adding – 'but Catherine, as I said, you are really going to have to do some serious training!'

'I will, Dad, I promise' replied Catherine, happily.

At this point Ian had two hugs from two delighted girls!

So the planning for the C2C 2 began. Ian quickly realised that booking B&B's and hotels for two girls and himself was going to be far more difficult than it had been previously so he made his bookings very early.

As to be expected as time passed by, Catherine began to have 'cold feet.' She is a lovely girl, very academic, a talented actress being part of the Penrith Players and she writes the most beautiful expressive and sensitive poetry and is a very caring child.

Our Coast to Coast Family – Rachael, Ian and Catherine Moseley.

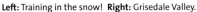

Left: Training in the snow! **Right:** Grisedale Valley.

Understandably Catherine approached the challenge of the C2C in a very different frame of mind from Rachael – she really does not enjoy walking a long way – it is just not her thing.

She voiced her fears to Ian.

'Dad, I'm not really sure that I can do the C2C – I do so **want** to walk with you and Rachael but it is such a long way!'

Ian explained that he had already booked all their accommodation, so she really did not have an option – but added, kindly,

'Everyone who takes on a big challenge, Catherine, feels exactly like you before they start. You will begin to feel much better when we start training – remember you promised to train!'

True to her word in the spring of 2012, Catherine began training with Rachael and Ian. All credit due to her for although she was somewhat reluctant at the beginning, she did train whenever the weather and time constraints allowed. She realised that she had made a commitment and really made a massive effort. At last, as she grew fitter, she thoroughly began to enjoy herself out on the fells and began to notice all the wonderful scenery and the nature around her just like Rachael.

One evening Ian heard them talking upstairs in their bedroom and Catherine, obviously, was still a little apprehensive about the challenge ahead.

'Don't worry, sis,' comforted Rachael, 'Daddy and I will help you all the way!' And they did!

A Memorable Training Day

Of all the training days, one particular Saturday in March stands out.

Ian had told the girls of his plan for training for the next day – a walk of about eight miles, full of interest with some necessary stiff climbs but breathtaking scenery. The route was to be through to Hartsop, up to the beautiful remote Hayeswater and onto The Knott with its spectacular views then back via lovely Angle Tarn and Boredale Hause to Old Water View.

Morning dawned and it had snowed overnight – a crisp, sunny morning with a clear, patchless blue sky! Initially both girls were reluctant to get up – they were just so warm and cosy snuggled down in their beds.

'Come on, you two,' urged Ian, 'just look out of the window!'

When they peered out, their reactions to the snow were completely different. Catherine was delighted because she thought that meant they wouldn't be able to walk. Wrong! Rachael was absolutely elated and couldn't wait to start.

All the way through Hartsop and up to Hayeswater, Rachael laughing merrily skipped ahead and Catherine followed with a very long, grumpy face! But when they reached Hayeswater everything changed for Catherine.

The view was stunning! There wasn't a single breath of wind and all the snow covered fells were mirrored perfectly in the still sparkling waters of the Reservoir. It was one of those absolutely unforgettable pictures you treasure forever!

Both girls just stared in wonderment at the incredible beauty of the scene in front of them – they were totally entranced! It was a superb place for them to

Beautiful Hayeswater.

have lunch so they all sat down on some rocks and munched away. When Ian suggested that it was time to carry on as they still had to climb up to the Knott, the enchantment of the water obviously continued. Because, although they had thought that they had already reached the summit, there were no complaints as they climbed happily – arm-in arm another 300' up the steep path to The Knott. Another fantastic, panoramic view greeted them.

As they descended to Angle Tarn, the girls had a competition to see who could do the highest star jump. Catherine won! A small but valuable confidence boosting triumph for her!

As they approached the tarn, both girls noticed another small frozen tarn just under Satura Crag, some three feet in front of them. Unfortunately, at that moment, Rachael tripped over some rocks, fell forwards and hit the ice with outstretched hands – there was big crack and the ice shattered and poor Rachael was plunged into the icy water up to her armpits! She was shocked by the cold but did not cry, not Rachael! Ian quickly picked her up, stripped her wet clothes off, dried her down and wrapped her up in some clean, spare clothes he had been carrying in his rucksack. Then he wrapped her up in his large fleece so that she was completely encased – just like in a cocoon! She was soon warm again!

'I'm okay now, thank you, Daddy', said Rachael with a grin, 'but I do look funny in this BIG fleece.'

Disaster averted, they both thoroughly enjoyed the rest of the walk home excitably pointing out things of interest like the tiny 'doll houses' of Patterdale far below them.

Left: Catherine's Star Jump. **Right:** Rachael's Star Jump.

Left: Angle Tarn – Big fleece – little walker! **Right:** 'Training is fun!'

They continued to chat about their amazing adventures that evening and agreed that it had been a wonderful training day after all!

Rachael, not to be outdone by her sister, practised her star jumps with such determination that on a different training day, she jumped so spectacularly high that she really appeared to be floating through the air!

Left: 'Come on, big sis – we'll do this together!' **Right:** Two pairs of boots being dipped in the Irish Sea.

St. Bees to Patterdale, C2C 2

Almost before they realised it, Rachael, Catherine and Ian were standing by Wainwright's Memorial that marks the beginning of the C2C at St. Bees. Photographs duly taken and they all went to dip their boots in the Irish Sea and Rachael and Catherine each selected a pebble which they were going to carry all the way – 192 miles – to Robin Hood's Bay so they could throw it into the North Sea. The weather was glorious, bright sunshine and really hot. They were both very excited! Catherine enthusiastically led the way up the cliffs towards the lighthouse just as Rachael had done a year ago.

Between St. Bees and Ennerdale, they began their 'Post Van Challenge.'

They had noticed, one day, that they had seen seven Post Office vans (or possibly the same van seven times!) so they decided that they would have a competition. The rules were that Rachael, Catherine and Ian each had to decide how many Post Office vans they would see before they reached the beach at Robin Hood's Bay. Catherine selected 23, Rachael 22 and Ian decided on 21. You will have to wait until the end of this C2C story, to find out who was the winner!

Throughout the Lake District section of the C2C, they followed the same plan as last year, walking out each day from Old Water View and returning each evening – with one exception.

Rachael had decided that she wanted to celebrate her 8th birthday back at her beloved Black Sail Hut in Ennerdale Valley, so Ian booked an overnight stay for the three of them. Having looked at the weather forecast, Ian decided to walk this section of the route in reverse (east to west). This was so they could walk across the high mountain route in the predicted nice weather and then drop down via Haystacks to Black Sail. The following day if bad weather

Left: 'From here we walk East all the way to Robin Hood's Bay!' **Right:** Honister Quarry.

'Nearly there! Hurray!' Can you spot Black Sail Hostel in the background?

Left: 'Happy 8th Birthday, Rachael!' **Right:** 'That was a great birthday!'

arrived as anticipated, they would be able to walk down the valley to Ennerdale Bridge with a gale blowing high above them in the mountains.

I was staying with them at Old Water View so I was able to drop them off at Honister Quarry and watched them excitably climb the steep, rocky path from the quarry to Fleetwith Pike fortified by large ice creams. In his rucksack Ian was carrying a surprise birthday cake, cards and presents as well as all their gear – after all, that is what daddies are for, isn't it!

Bless her! Rachael soon ran out of energy as she had really been really poorly with the usual 'school stomach bug' and was still quite weak. She sank down, exhausted, on a rock near the path. But nothing stops that little girl for long – a few words of encouragement from Catherine and Daddy and several drinks and she was up on her feet again. Eager to help, Catherine, very kindly, carried Rachael's rucksack! Sheer determination got Rachael to Black Sail where she had a huge surprise!

Birthday balloons were bobbing merrily outside the hut! Actually they had been put up to celebrate the warden's birthday the day before but naturally Rachael thought they were for her! It was just the boost she needed. Soon she was racing around with Catherine, tummy-ache forgotten, jumping and laughing in sheer joy – both of them were absolutely elated! Ian was delighted to see that Catherine clearly loved Black Sail as much as we all do!

The warden blew up some more special balloons just for Rachael and cooked a delicious meal for everyone. Fortunately another family was staying at Black Sail so they all shared Rachael's birthday cake and had a fantastic time! What a wonderful, memorable way for Rachael to celebrate her eighth birthday!

The next day they all walked happily together in fleeting sunshine down the long forest road towards Ennerdale Bridge. Rachael was sporting two balloons tied to her rucksack and because, devoid of the birthday cake, Daddy's rucksack looked too small, Catherine and Rachael stuffed another balloon inside his rucksack making it look impressively large and heavy! The girls skipped for joy hand-in hand most of the way so they hardly noticed just how long that track is. As anticipated, there was indeed a gale blowing high above them in the mountains.

I picked them up just outside Ennerdale Bridge and took them home to Old Water View. They chatted excitedly all the way full of their wonderful experience!

Patterdale to Shap

Their first attempt to reach Shap from Old Water View was memorable for all the wrong reasons!

The weather was forecasted to be fine with periods of sunshine but with the warning that it would become increasingly windy by late afternoon. Ian had an important decision to make – should he take Rachael and Catherine on the high route which climbs up to the Hause and then to the picturesque Angle Tarn and up again over The Knott and Kidsty Pike and down to Haweswater, a fabulous scenic route to Shap or should they go by a lower route – it was really a 50/50 decision.

Ian has a fantastic knowledge of all the varied weather conditions and routes in the Lake District and especially this section as he is constantly asked for advice by walkers staying at Old Water View. After much deliberation and knowing that if the weather forecast was correct, they would be over the high ground and down by Haweswater by the time the predicted winds came, Ian decided on the high route.

In good spirits, they set off in lovely sunshine – it was going to be a really great fun day or so they thought! They climbed steadily with the girls taking it in turn to lead but as they trudged up towards Satura Crag, having admired the breath-taking beauty of Angle Tarn, the wind suddenly rose and huge gusts battered them.

The situation rapidly became very dangerous. Soon all of them even Ian, were having problems staying on their feet and poor Rachael was blown over several times. Catherine had to cling desperately to Daddy as well. It was obvious that they could not carry on safely so Ian turned them round intending to aim for the comparative shelter of the rocks around Angle Tarn some way below. Fortunately as they descended carefully, fearfully holding on to each other, the swirling, gusting wind was blowing them in towards the mountain which, truly, was a lifesaver as at this point there is a dangerous drop to the left.

However Ian knew from his wide experience that the direction of the wind could change in an instant, then their situation could become perilous. They crouched down under some rocks by Angle Tarn in comparative safety but they were stuck! For the moment, they could neither go up to the Knott nor

Still smiling at the end of that day!

down to Patterdale. The girls were very scared but immensely comforted by the presence of their Daddy – they knew he would keep them safe.

When there was a slight lull in the severity of the wind, Ian managed to phone Old Water View and told a friend there that he was aborting the day's walk and they were all coming home via Martindale. Fortunately Ian knew of a rarely used path that descended through Martindale so they crawled over the intervening ridge and down this path. Now, at last, they were out of that frightening wind but as walkers in the Lakes will know, just when you think you have won, you are always surprised. With a last 'Hurrah!' a sudden gust of wind lifted Rachael up and deposited her gently on her bottom – she was not amused!

That brave little girl, for once, was still scared, as to a degree was Catherine. They were both afraid that the dreadful wind would come back and batter them again. Reassured by Ian, they made their way down to Martindale Church where Ian's friend picked them up and took them home to Old Water View. By this time, unbelievably, they were both eager to undertake another attempt the next day.

True walkers – all three!

Second attempt to reach Shap

So a day behind schedule, they planned their second assault on Shap! However the weather made the high route totally impossible. The cloud base was extremely low, the winds were high and rain poured down from black clouds encircling Kidsty Pike. Place Fell and Boredale Hause were completely invisible from Patterdale.

Not to be deterred but mindful of their previous frightening day on that section, Ian decided to stay safe and follow Wainwright's advice about such conditions and take the 'Winter Route'. From Pooley Bridge a well-marked path heads over Askham Fell, a comparatively low stretch of moorland, to the quiet, picturesque lane that leads into Bampton Grange, four miles from Shap, and their destination for that day.

As they looked back at Patterdale from the northern end of Ullswater, they were amazed to see just how localised the threatening weather really was – heavy black clouds hung over the whole of Patterdale and Glenridding completely covering all of the high fells. Yet, ironically, Rachael, Catherine and Ian walked the 'Winter Route' in bright sunshine – in fact it was so hot that they walked in T-shirts and had to use sun-block cream! The vagaries of the capricious Lake District weather!

From Bampton Grange, they were picked up again and transported back to Old Water View.

Bampton Grange to Orton

Next day, they were dropped off near the church at Bampton Grange where they had ended their previous walk and continued their journey through Shap and on to Orton. The girls were fascinated to find the route then crossed a bridge over a train-line especially Rachael, who, if you remember had an unpleasant experience crossing railway lines in her first C2C. All the time there was the increasing noise of the motorway as they neared yet another bridge which crosses the M6. Both Rachael and Catherine spent considerable time leaning on this bridge thoroughly engrossed in watching the trucks thundering underneath and the cars whizzing past. They waved enthusiastically to everyone and got several waves from drivers in return.

Unaccountably there was a sleeping bag and belongings on the steps leading to the bridge – clearly there had been someone sleeping rough there – but why? It really was a mystery because the steps were in a very exposed, cold and noisy position so why would anyone chose to sleep there when nearby in Shap or beyond on the way to Orton, there was plenty of shelter.

Left: Crossing the noisy M6. **Right:** 'Look! Rachael has 'bunny ears!'

'We've earned our chocolate, Dad!'

They never did find out – there was no sign whatsoever of the owner of the sleeping bag.

The girls were ready to have their lunch but Ian, sensibly, made them wait until the obtrusive sounds of the motorway had disappeared. Now they were on the limestone plateau of Orton Scar – Rachael in particular, was enthralled by the changes in the landscape. They discovered the stone circle near Oddendale – not easy to find – and then Rachael spotted two large rocks which Wainwright sketches in his famous C2C Book as interesting 'granite erratic boulders resting on limestone'. She, however, remembered them for a very different reason,

'Come on, Catherine,' she cried, 'let me show you where I had a wee last year!' Catherine was not impressed!

Then they found Robin Hood's Grave – it's amazing just how many places that errant outlaw is buried. Here they turned right and walked down through the fields to Orton that quintessential English village with its sparkling stream, ducks and duck pond and beautiful village green. More importantly, it has a Chocolate Factory – Catherine was especially thrilled as she hadn't believed Ian or Rachael when they'd told her about it. She had thought that they were just encouraging her to keep going!

Happily Catherine and Rachael both rushed in to buy well-deserved rewards. They each selected a white lollipop thinking it was made of white chocolate – well you would, wouldn't you? A chocolate factory should only make chocolate sweets! Unfortunately, no! The lollipops were made of white rock! But there is a bonus in everything if you seek it – the lollipops lasted for ages and kept them quiet all the way home.

Orton to Kirkby Stephen

I drove Rachael, Catherine and Ian back to Orton the next day. From here they would be following the pattern of the previous year and staying at B&B's and hotels all the way through to Robin Hood's Bay.

We had a bit of a disastrous start. After packing the previous evening, Ian had discovered that new socks were needed for everyone so we had to drive to Penrith first. However when Ian checked that the girls had their boots, Rachael discovered that hers were still back at Old Water View – oh dear! What a disaster! That meant a long, twisting drive back home and both girls felt car sick. Boots retrieved, we set off again but the extra driving was too much for delicate stomachs – both Rachael and Catherine were sick – poor Catherine especially so!

In fact when I dropped them off at the Chocolate Factory at Orton neither of them even mentioned buying any chocolate!

I kissed the girls, gave them a hug and waved them 'Goodbye' and took their luggage on to Fletcher House in Kirkby Stephen, their destination that evening. As last year, Packhorse would be transporting their heavy bags for free through to Robin Hood's Bay. As you may well imagine, with two girls, there was a little more luggage than the previous year and yes! This time, Ian did remember to pack enough shirts for himself!

Due to their sickness, both girls really struggled this day, particularly Catherine who had been sick so many times, she had absolutely no energy left. Fortunately the weather was glorious which helped a lot and both girls cheered up as they sat on some rocks by the reedy Sunbiggin Tarn to have their lunch.

In fact – Rachael wrote in her diary that evening 'I really think this is a beautiful walk – Sunbiggin Tarn is lovely!'

Left: A windy break at Sunbiggin Tarn. **Right:** Our B&B at Kirkby Stephen.

They all went to same pub in Kirkby Stephen where Rachael and Catherine played happily in the same sandpit and had a little competition to see who could build the best sandcastle. Daddy watched fondly from the garden having treated himself to two beers!

On to Keld

This year the reports of the conditions on Nine Standards Rigg were even worse than last year. At Old Water View, Ian had heard that one unlucky man had sunk up to his waist in the deep sticky peat and had to be rescued so there was no question of Ian and the girls using that dangerous route. Instead they followed the road route again but this year in pleasant weather – no mist or rain.

By now Rachel was back to her usual bouncy, happy self and skipped merrily ahead constantly discovering simple things of interest on the way – varieties of flowers, the shape of a bush, fleeting clouds and listening enthralled to birdsongs.

But poor Catherine, still not fully recovered, was struggling – head down she was trudging doggedly at about half of her normal walking pace – seeing nothing! Afterwards she described this as her most difficult day. When they approached a quite long but fairly gradual climb, Catherine looked at this hill with horror – in her notes she described it as 'a massive, gigantic hill!'

Somehow Ian had to get her to the top. At this point, on the right hand side of the road, there are snow poles, some three metres high. To encourage Catherine to carry on, Ian, cleverly, invented the 'Post to Post Walk' – he set Catherine the small target of walking from one post to the next and then urged her to tackle reaching the next post. In this gruelling way they slowly progressed

Left: The joy of flowers! **Right:** 'Keld at last and half-way!'

to the top of the hill where Catherine sank down completely exhausted.

After lunch, Catherine was still feeling shattered and clearly just hated every step of the way. To cheer her up, Ian decided to have a little fun with her – Keld Lodge, their destination, was actually only a few hundred yards away but Ian thought if he could convince Catherine that there still was a long way to go, he could then surprise her when he revealed that Keld Lodge was just ahead. Joke! No! His plan backfired – badly!

Because when he pointed to a barn miles away on the horizon and told Catherine that was Keld Lodge he had expected her just to grumble but no – Catherine burst into tears and sobbed! Totally distraught! Ian felt dreadful – he had completely misread the situation because normally Catherine has a fantastic sense of humour. But the result showed how worn out she really was – bless her! Ian apologised quickly and gave her a huge hug and after seeing that they were almost at Keld Lodge, Catherine's tears soon dried up.

They had a super evening there and after a delicious meal, Catherine was feeling much better and eager to continue their walk the next day so much so that when Ian gave her the option of stopping and going home, she refused,

'No Daddy, I want to walk with you all the way,' she said.

She had endured a lot that day – but come through all that darkness and had emerged into the light! Ian was truly impressed by her achievements and very proud of her too. Now, he had two determined walkers with him – Rachael and Catherine – what a lucky Daddy!

In her diary Catherine had written that Keld Lodge was her favourite overnight stay.

The following morning in good spirits, both girls posed giggling, for photos in front of the sign for 'Butt House' – they found the name highly amusing for some reason – I wonder what it was?

Catrake Force – Keld.

As Rachael had been, Catherine too was entranced by the beautiful waterfalls where the C2C crosses the Pennine Way.

Rachael exclaimed, 'me and dad are going to come back one day and walk the Pennine Way!'

'Well you won't have ME with you!' stated Catherine emphatically!

Keld to Reeth

They followed the beautiful River Swale with its sparkling waterfalls all the way to Reeth. It is the most picturesque walk with graceful trees, lovely springy grass and the music of the bubbling water. Catherine, like Rachael was enchanted.

They soon met up with a gentleman from Holland who introduced himself as 'Kees' – pronounced 'Case'. Ian thought that he looked familiar but couldn't remember where they had met – then he realised that Kees had been a guest recently at Old Water View and Ian had actually served him with his dinner and breakfast! Kees was doing the C2C too and was truly impressed by the performance of the girls – he could hardly believe just how far they had walked. To celebrate, he gave them both souvenir key rings made of two miniature clogs to fasten on their backpacks. They were thrilled!

Kees was to walk with them most of the way to Robin Hood's Bay and he helped a great deal especially encouraging Catherine when, inevitably, she had some really low points. He just dropped back, quite naturally, when she was trailing behind and chatted to her companionably and this really spurred her on.

Kees, if you read this – we thank you so much for helping Catherine to achieve an amazing personal challenge at just ten years old!

Rachael was keen to have their lunch at the King's Head at Gunnerside because she remembered a very friendly cat called Sid that lived at the pub. So they sat outside eating their lunches – Ian had a beer and the girls some chocolate and chocolate drinks like Rachael's double chocolate hit of last year. Both girls were very pleased to see that the cat was still there, scrounging food and begging as usual! He got several treats!

They continued along the Swale until they reached Springfield House – where the lovely B&B owners were absolutely delighted to meet Catherine and amazed that Rachael was doing the C2C again so soon!

As they set out for Richmond next morning, both girls got a huge hug and a cheery 'Good-bye and Good Luck!'

Reeth to Richmond

Shortly after Marrick Priory, there is quite a steep climb up through Whitcliffe Wood – Catherine was filled with dismay and looked very cross.

'It took 101 steps to climb up here, Dad!' she protested when at last she reached the top, 'I hope there aren't any more big hills!'

Apart from this small incident, the remainder of their walk to Richmond was uneventful at least as far as walking was concerned but memorable for several 'accidents'.

The first was Catherine's 'demolition' attempt on an ancient monument!

Wainwright described it as 'a prominent white cairn' and is a spot just past Clapgate Beck where many C2Coasters have a rest before carrying on to Richmond. Catherine, truly, just put one finger on it and a big stone fell down from it with a resounding thud and rolled along the ground! Whoops! Catherine was horrified and very embarrassed because she had a big audience of walkers who were really amused! Quickly Ian helped her to stuff it back a leaving the ancient monument more or less as it had been.

However they couldn't escape immediately because the group of C2Coasters were so thrilled to meet two such amazing little walkers that they all wanted to pose for photos with the girls. After this, Rachael, Catherine and Ian swiftly left the scene before any more disasters happened!

However Rachael was desperate for a wee and dashed behind some hay bales! Fortunately there was no-one to see her pink cap appearing over the hay so thankfully another potentially embarrassing 'accident' was averted. Ian was quite grateful when at last they reached Richmond!

But as everyone knows, 'accidents' are said to come in threes – and they did!

Left: 'Cheers! We're at Richmond!' **Right:** Just before Rachael's pizza went splat on the floor!

That evening all three tucked into tasty takeaway pizza and chips sitting in the picturesque market square in Richmond. Rachael had two pizzas – as her first one fell splat, face-down on the ground!

Richmond to Danby Whiske

Danby Whiske was their next target. Ian bought the girls huge ice-creams to help them on their way (a rare treat at 9am but they deserved it!). The route is not difficult on this stretch so Ian took the opportunity to teach Catherine some map-reading skills as he had done for Rachael last year. She navigated successfully through endless fields – some of them full of golden waving corn higher than our intrepid little walkers!

Rachael's entry in her diary at the end of the day was,

'I'm tired but very happy!'

Catherine cheerfully agreed – she had learned a new, valuable skill and was proud of herself.

Danby Whiske to Ingleby Cross

Remember the farmer who clearly did not like walkers? Well this year he had increased his plastic deterrents on the stile – the skull was still there but the number of rats had increased to three (I didn't know that plastic rats could breed, did you?) and there were now three plastic owls! Both girls were not deterred but highly amused and posed for lots of photos.

At Ingleby Cross Rachael introduced Catherine to her statue of 'The Chain Lady' outside The Bluebell Inn – more photos, of course.

Three Wise Monkeys?

Like last year, they spent a wonderful evening with Ian's friends, Ruth and Gerry. The girls were delighted and they played happily with all three dogs in the garden. Leader got a special cuddle from both of them. After another delicious meal, when they were relaxing in the garden watching the girls so happy and contented, Ian reflected on just how lucky he was to have two such wonderful girls and to be sharing the fantastic challenge of the C2C with them.

Ingleby Cross to Clay Bank Top

Next morning, actually the first morning of the Olympic Games, the girls were rudely awakened at 5am by Ian, fully dressed, shaking them and exclaiming,
    'Come on, Lazybones, get up! It's 7am already!'
    Rachael leapt out of bed and was soon half-dressed when Catherine, still in bed, looked at her watch and then at Ian and protested with an emphatic voice,
    'But Dad, look at my watch and check it with yours – it is only 5am!'
    Ian had to admit that this was true but not wanting to lose face, he added,' our watches could be wrong!'
    Sensibly Catherine switched on the TV and sure enough it was still only just past 5am! She smugly snuggled comfortably down her cosy bed while Rachael and Ian had to undress! Back to sleep for another two hours!

Fortunately the weather that morning was brilliant, warm sunshine and just a gentle breeze – ideal for walking so the girls did forgive Ian – after all even 'perfect' dads can make mistakes! (Actually Ian had relied on the B&B clock in his bedroom which was two hours fast!).

They climbed up to Carlton Bank and followed the paved path over the moors. The clear views were breathtaking and far reaching – both girls were spellbound as they paused frequently to point out different interesting features below the ridge and far ahead. By now Catherine was finding the walking easier and marched happily along – possibly motivated by her first glimpse of the North Sea!

They were very disappointed to find that Lord's Stone Café, that haven for so many walkers, had closed down. Rachael had kept telling Catherine that there was a sofa on the top of Cringle End as did Ian. Catherine did not believe them – she just thought that they saying that so she would not grumble when she had to climb that steep path. But sure enough, the large stone seat was there and both girls really enjoyed posing bathed in sunshine for several photos and admiring the fantastic views. They continued over Cringle Moor and the summit of Cold Moor and stopped to have their lunch near the top of Hasty Bank before they tackled the winding, steep descent to the enclosures on the saddle between Hasty Bank and the challenging Wainstones!

Glad for a rest, they settled themselves comfortably on some rocks and munched away merrily. Then Catherine dropped her apple! Ian and Catherine watched it bouncing rapidly down the twisting path with Rachael in hot pursuit! As you would expect, eventually she caught it and carried it triumphantly back up to Catherine who thanked her gratefully – and yes, after a quick wipe and in spite of the obvious bruising, she ate it hungrily!

From where they were sitting, they could see a herd of probably around thirty Galloway cattle milling around the gate of the enclosures far below. It was a gate they had to use. All the way down, Ian schooled them about how they must behave as Galloway's have a reputation for being quite awkward – they must approach the cows steadily and quietly, not a single sound! Bless them, they obeyed to the letter!

Then as they were in the middle of the herd, potentially the most dangerous place, Ian's mobile rang! (Sorry! I'm afraid the culprit was me, Grandma Joyce, just phoning to see if they were okay – the girls have reminded me frequently about this!). Ian quickly hit the silence button and fortunately the cows just looked nonplussed and carried on eating. Disaster averted!

Thankfully they climbed up to the spectacular Wainstones. As Rachael had been last year, Catherine was completely overcome by the incredible shapes and natural sculptures of the rocks. Excitably, they climbed over them, posed by them and jumped from them. They were in heaven! Two gloriously happy girls! Ian's camera never stopped clicking!

They descended to Clay Bank Top where the road, the B1257, runs over a considerable hill between Chop Gate (their destination) and Great Broughton some two miles away! At this point, Ian remembered that the small B&B where

A sofa in the clouds for two.

Left and right: The amazing Wainstones.

Catherine, Rachael, Rob and Nelly.

they stayed last year did not take bank cards so he needed some cash. He knew that there was a shop with a Post Office at Great Broughton so instead of just turning right to walk down to Chop Gate they had to turn left and descend two miles to Great Broughton which with the return journey added an extra four miles to their day.

The girls were not impressed – they had already done a long tough walk so they were really looking forward to some rewards when they finally reached the shop – possibly ice creams and sweets! They were all to be disappointed because the Post Office part of the shop had closed, so no cash and the shop shelves were almost empty. No cash, no sweets and no ice creams! Embarrassed the girl behind the counter explained that the owner was away and she had not been able to stock up.

The girls were not happy! Ian stopped at a nearby pub and bought them a drink but again there were no sweets and not even crisps! Things were not going well and to add to their problems it started to pour down with typical Lakeland style rain – incessant!

Soon they were all soaked! Actually Rachael didn't mind, ever cheerful she just skipped along completely oblivious of the rain – so quickly in fact that she reached the Chop Gate sign and waited there merrily chasing raindrops until about twenty minutes later, Catherine trudged miserably down to join her. Catherine was absolutely soaked – her face was a picture! Ian tried hard not to smile.

When they finally arrived at Rachael and Ian's favourite B&B, Forge House, Rob and Jenny made a huge pot of tea and big cups of hot chocolate for the girls.

'Hanging out' at Blowarth Junction.

After a lovely hot shower, Catherine cheered up and graciously forgave Ian! At the local pub, they all had a substantial, delicious meal which tasted even better for knowing that they had thoroughly earned it!

Next morning, Rob and Jenny took the girls to their smallholding and let them feed the chickens, goats, sheep and their cows Nelly and Doris and the bull calf called Gismo!

They were completely engrossed and did a very good job and this time, both girls, were able to sit on Nelly.

Afterwards Rob and Jenny gave them a lift to the nearest town where Ian was able to withdraw some cash and pay their bill. Then they dropped Ian and the girls off back at Clay Bank Top at the beginning of that day's walk.

Catherine and Rachael, with superior looks on their faces, did point out that, thanks to dad, this was their third visit to Clay Bank Top in less than 24 hours!

Clay Bank Top through Blowarth Junction to The Lion Inn

It was a lovely day as they crossed Urra Moor although the heather wasn't quite out, the vast panoramic views kept the girls interested. Not far from Blowarth Junction where they would join the cinder track of the former Rosedale Ironstone Railway, they paused for photos beside the trig point on the tumulus at the summit of Urra Moor. This marks the highest point of the Cleveland Hills. Of course, the girls had to climb the trig point too so they were the highest.

Left: Saved by a modern 'Sir Walter Raleigh!' **Right:** 'Fat Betty' – Guess what Rachael hid here!

At Blowarth Junction the route of the Cleveland Way turns north so now they were following the route of the famous Lyke Wake Walk all the way to The Lion Inn. Beside the path, there were lots of clucking, angry grouse trying desperately to hide in the heather. If you remember last year Ian and Rachael had adopted the grouse as their favourite bird! This year Catherine added her efforts to Rachael's to try to catch at least one grouse but yet again both girls were unsuccessful! Not even a feather was caught! However they did have a lovely treat – lots of enchanting tiny baby grouse were scuttling along the cinder path – obviously it was far easier for them to walk here than in the deep heather! Both girls, completely absorbed, watched them quietly.

Rachael was the first to spot the remote Lion Inn in the distance – not far to go now!

However before they reached it – for no apparent reason– there was about a six foot stretch of the path that somehow had been churned up resulting in a deep, muddy morass that you simply could not cross without sinking in so deep that it would be over your boots. Ian searched in the deep heather both sides of the path and found large, heavy flat boulder. Ever the knight in shining armour, Ian dropped the stone in the middle of the mud where it made a perfect stepping stone for the girls and future walkers – a modern Sir Walter Raleigh! (Of course it meant that he didn't get his shoes muddy either!).

Here Rachael said for the first time,

'I wonder of it will still be there when we come again next year?' Ian and Catherine didn't respond, they just ignored her because there would be no C2C next year (Ian was adamant about that!).

That evening at dinner, Ian played another trick on Catherine – he doesn't learn does he?

When she went outside to answer a phone call from her mum, Ian noticed that although she had only eaten a quarter of the dessert, the ice cream on her Banana Split had begun to melt. So just to help out, he quickly ate the remains of her dessert! You can imagine the look on her face when she returned to find an empty bowl – disgust doesn't describe it – she had earned that treat!

'Dad how could you!' she protested angrily.

Of course Ian wasn't that cruel – he produced another large Banana Split as if by magic! He had already bought her another one and hidden it!

'Naughty Dad!' she said forgivingly, 'you do like your silly jokes, don't you!'

This was said in the kind of voice that all parents will recognise when you feel like the child and your child is the mature adult!

Next morning as they walked along the road from the Lion Inn up to Fat Betty on Rosedale Head, Catherine noticed that the local farmers had placed 'SLOW DOWN' signs on the side of the road. Although they had done this to warn motorists that there were lots of lambs around, Catherine was convinced that the signs were to slow Rachael down so she could keep up with her! Bless her!

At Fat Betty naturally they posed for yet more photos and left one of their chocolate bars and picked up the one left on this monument. This is a tradition of the C2C Walk.

They marched on thoroughly enjoying the walk to the Cross on Fryup Head. Here Rachael asked Ian for 20p and promptly buried it at the base of the monument.

'What are you doing?' asked Ian.

'I'm burying it to see if it is still there when we come again next year!' Rachael, clearly was not going to be ignored.

This time, Ian responded firmly, 'We are not coming back that soon! There will be no C2C in 2013!'

Then he added,

'Well, I suppose that as you have buried it so well and no-one will think to look there, your 20p could still be waiting for you if we do come back again several years from now. But definitely not in 2013!'

Rachael, of course, had other ideas! Catherine said nothing as she knew something that Dad did not know… Rachael had already buried another coin under Fat Betty as double insurance. A little girl with a mission!

'Ready for our ride on the steam train'.

Fryup Monument to beyond Grosmont

From one horizon to another, they could see the rain really pouring down all around them from huge threatening black clouds, but luckily Ian and the girls were able to follow the broad grassy track past Trough House, a shooting lodge, in a 'bubble of perfect sunshine!'

When they reached the station at Glaisdale, they found a discarded road sign in the hedgerow, obviously left behind from road works. On the big red sign in large white letters was 'SLOW'. With a smile, Rachael and Ian awarded it to Catherine for being a slow walker. She saw the funny side of the gesture (I told you that she had a good sense of humour) and insisted that Ian took a photo of her proudly holding the sign.

From here they walked on through Egton Bridge and reached Grosmont so early that they decided to treat themselves to a ride on the fantastic steam train to Goathland – which readers who are fans of the TV series 'Heartbeat' will know as the village of Aidensfield. After an interesting walk around and armed with their choice of sweets, they boarded the steam train back to Grosmont.

There is a small but well-stocked book shop near the train station which has lots of books particularly about steam trains, the C2C and the North York

Moors etc. Knowing how much academic Catherine loves to read, Ian gave her some money to buy a book. You will never guess what she bought – she came out with a huge grin on her face with a book called – 'How to train a boy!' Had she Ian in mind, one wonders? You will soon find out!

They took the bus back to the same B&B as last year in Glaisdale as they had walked about four miles past their planned finishing point for the day.

That evening both girls could hardly wait to go to the local pub because Rachael had told Catherine about the massive pizza and chips she had eaten there the year before. Tragedy! They did not serve pizzas anymore, so the girls had to settle for a very tasty vegetarian meal but were really disappointed that it was not the famed massive pizza!

Grosmont to Robin Hood's Bay – their ultimate destination!

Next day they took the train back to Grosmont. Rachael was adamant that they must start from the exact spot they had reached yesterday – she did not intend anyone to be able to accuse her of missing a single step of the C2C 2.

Of course then they faced that steep, endless – one in three – hill! (Later christened by Rachael 'The Huff & Puff Hill').

Catherine's face was a picture of disbelief and astonishment!

'Dad, I thought that all the hills were behind us! You didn't tell me about this one!'

Ian thought it better not to answer but Rachael added thinking of last year, 'And where is Trish when you want her!'

Eventually they conquered the hill and reached the open moor beyond. As they were all walking down to Littlebeck with Ian was about twenty feet in front of the girls who were walking arm-in-arm, he heard a lot of giggling behind him. At first Ian thought that it was just the girls having fun but then he picked up exactly what they were giggling about and realised that they were plotting.

Their conversation went something like this,

Rachael: 'Catherine, how can I convince Dad to do this again with me. I really, really want to do a hat trick of C2Cs. You have to help me to find a way of doing it with dad again next year, please!'

'Why would you want to do it again – it is a nightmare! You must be mad!' replied Catherine giggling and added, 'you have absolutely no chance – you only got to do the C2C again this year because I was jealous and wanted to do it like you and now I wish I hadn't! My poor feet are positively killing me!'

(Actually neither girl ever had a single blister!).

Between them they obviously hatched a cunning plan – perhaps that book gave them some ideas.

The plotting begins!

About ten minutes later came the ambush. They caught up with Ian and walked very close to him – one either side. As she gazed up into Ian's face, donning her most appealing, sorrowful look, Rachael said,

'Daddy, you are being really mean and unfair to me and it's not very nice!'

Astonished Ian replied,' Why! What have I done?'

'Well!' came Rachael's response, ' You know that all the people who do the C2C when they have thrown their pebble into the sea and wet their boots – they get to stay overnight at a B&B, meet up in the pub and celebrate their success and we don't get to stay overnight, so that is why it isn't fair!'

Good tactics – just wait for the rest of the master plan!

She continued after a suitable pregnant pause for her previous words to sink in,

'I know just how you can make it up to me.'

Ian waited silently well aware that he was being manipulated.

'You know how you let me celebrate my eighth birthday at Black Sail this year; well I really, really want to celebrate my ninth birthday in a B&B at Robin Hood's Bay, please!'

'That seems a reasonable request,' answered Ian smiling, 'Yes, you can have your ninth birthday at Robin Hood's Bay, I promise!'

On hearing this promise, Rachael said excitably, 'Wow, Catherine! You see dad has just agreed that I can spend my ninth birthday in a B&B at Robin Hood's Bay. He just doesn't know yet that we are going to be walking all the way there from St. Bees!'

'Well, he does now!' Catherine pointed out with a huge grin.

Fylingthorpe 1½
Robin Hood's Bay 2

Scarboro' 15 A171   Whitby 6 A171

638C

'Nearly there and we've outwitted Dad!'

Every sensible dad knows when he has been beaten – what could he say?

'I have been out-manoeuvred by two experts,' Ian thought, ' and they are only eight and ten – the future is going to be very interesting!'

Just beyond Littlebeck they spotted another little red post van – this made the 21st van spotted on the whole trip! As you may remember, Ian, at the start of the Post Van Challenge, had chosen 21, Rachael 22 and Catherine 23. So, as he knew there was only just over another road mile to walk before Robin Hood's Bay, Ian was confident that he would win and said so smugly!

Suspecting that Ian had somehow adjusted the rules to suit himself, they girls again came up with a plan to defeat him. Rachael suggested that it would be very nice to go a different way from last year – not over the cliffs but by the fields (from which the road was visible) and then actually follow the road into Robin Hood's Bay – Catherine agreed enthusiastically. I'm sure you can understand their cunning plan – yes! More road walking and more chance of seeing red post vans!

When Ian spotted a road sign saying Robin Hood's Bay – half a mile – he pointed to it and said proudly,

'There – only half a mile to go – you've no chance either of you – I've won!'

What do they say about pride coming before a fall – it did. Just as he was proclaiming his victory, a red post van came round the corner! Number 22 so Rachael had won – she laughed her head off!

Poor Catherine, however, was quite upset and moaned,

'It's not fair! I can't beat my sister at anything no matter what I do or how hard I try!'

Job done! Throwing our pebbles into the North Sea.

However the fates decreed otherwise because five minutes later, just as they reached the sign for Robin Hood's Bay, another red post van came past – number 23. Catherine had won – she was ecstatic and marched through the village to the top of the steep hill that leads down to the beach with an enormous grin on her face – not because she had almost finished the C2C – oh no! Because at last she had beaten Rachael and Ian as well!

Then the girls reminded Ian that one of his rules had been that the person who lost by the most bought the ice creams – of course that was Ian so he bought them both a huge ice cream cone.

Rachael raced down the hill and onto the beach, shouting for sheer joy with arms outstretched – 'I've done it, I've done it again!'

Catherine trudged down more sedately but soon joined her sister. Ian said that you could see she was really happy and quietly proud of herself – she had overcome all her problems and fears and succeeded – she had achieved her goal – she had walked the C2C at ten years old! A fantastic achievement for her and one, hopefully, she will remember with pride forever! We certainly will!

Full of joy, together two delighted girls threw their pebbles into the North Sea and jumped excitably into the waves. Then they went into Wainwright's Bar to sign the register and Ian bought them all a well-deserved drink! Sitting outside, Catherine and Rachael chatted happily about their amazing experiences.

'Two down – one to go – still working on Dad!'

Ian, a very proud dad, listened to them fondly and reflected on what had been a challenging but unforgettable C2C – what stars his girls were – life was very good!

At one point, Rachael said thoughtfully,

'You know what would have been absolutely brilliant, Daddy – we should have carried your Olympic Torch with us all the way!'

'Why?' Ian asked, somewhat puzzled.

Rachael explained slowly and patiently,

'Because we are going to celebrate my ninth birthday here at Robin Hood's Bay next year, aren't we?

And remember, Daddy, earlier this summer, you carried your Olympic Torch through the Lake District part near to St. Bees on Catherine's tenth birthday so if we had it here now, it would be like celebrating her birthday again at Robin Hood's Bay, wouldn't it?'

'Actually there is some logic somewhere in that explanation,' mused Ian but didn't say anything because he knew who would have been carrying the Torch all the way and anyway it was too late for this year!

Ian had phoned ahead and arranged with Packhorse to give them a free lift home to Old Water View. The only problem was they had to climb back up the steep hill so they could be picked up! You can imagine Catherine's face when she heard that,

'Oh no!' she protested – 'Not climbing again – I don't believe it!'

'Well done both of you!' (Wait until you see the back of Rachael's shirt!)

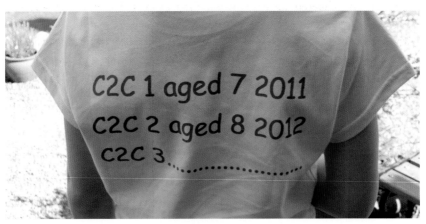

'Mission Accomplished! Just the date of my C2C 3 needed now!'

A little while after their remarkable C2C 2, Rachael and Catherine received a lovely surprise present from Kees – a handwritten letter and pair of hand made clogs each. They were specially made for the girls by one of the last traditional clog makers in The Netherlands and hand painted with a C2C logo by his wife.

The girls were delighted! Ian has all these proudly displayed in his Wainwright's Bar at Old Water View. Should readers stay with Ian in the future, they will be able to see these wonderful souvenirs of an inspirational C2C 2. Many C2Coasters have done so already but none can fit in them!

Coast to Coast 3 – 2013!

Coast to Coast 3 – the walk that definitely was not going to happen!

About two weeks after getting back from the C2C 2, Ian added up what Rachael and Catherine had raised in sponsorship for their school in Patterdale and The Patterdale Mountain Rescue Team.

At this point it was a magnificent £3,350 so Rachael, Catherine and Ian walked down to the Mountain Rescue Centre to donate a welcome cheque for £1,000 to the team.

All the members made a terrific fuss of the girls, thanking them profusely.

Rachael asked when she could become a Mountain Rescue Team member and was a little disappointed to be told that she was a bit too young and that you have to be at least 16 years old because the rescue work can be very dangerous. However, she cheered up a lot when they promised that if she was still interested when she was 14, she could go and train with them! Wow! Training with that famous rescue team would be awesome and not too long to wait!

There was better news to come! In October 2012, Rachael received a letter from The Patterdale Mountain Rescue Team making her a life-time member of their Supporters' Club! She was ecstatic! Her proud dad, Ian, framed it and it is hanging in his wonderful Wainwright's Bar at Old Water View.

The surprises did not end there for this brave and inspirational little walker. At Christmas, members of the Patterdale team gave her a special Mountain Rescue Team jacket and a warm base-layer shirt!

She was absolutely delighted and exclaimed,

'Now I feel a proper member! Thank you! Thank you so much! I just love them – I'll wear them all the time!' And she did!

Of course she would also wear this wonderful 'uniform' on her C2C 3 – she was so proud!

As you may have guessed, Ian had admitted defeat and had booked all the B&Bs along the C2C again. How could he deny his incredible little walker the chance to become a record breaker! He planned their C2C 3 to coincide with the early Easter holidays in 2013. They would walk together for 17 days and, magically, would reach Robin Hood's Bay on Rachael's ninth birthday, just as she wanted! Well she'd earned that treat hadn't she?

She had another Christmas present to help her on her way. I had bought her a special mascot – a little bear proudly sporting a red jumper just like the

I want to be in Mountain Rescue when I grow up!

mascot I had taken that September when I trekked in the Himalayas. However this bear had special gold embroidery on his red jumper.

On the front it said … 'RACHAEL C2C 3 2013' and on the back it said 'with my Dad'. Rachael named her bear 'WILLY'.

Rachael was overjoyed and so excited – the end of March would soon come and she could start her C2C 3 challenge!

Very soon Ian was shopping for kit (kit for the C2C that he was never going to do again at least for several years!) By now, of course Rachael was older and had definite ideas as to what she wanted so shopping wasn't quite as easy as Ian had anticipated. However she listened sensibly to what her dad said was suitable – after all she was an experienced walker now!

What Rachael did not know was that I had planned an extra surprise for her when she stopped at her beloved Black Sail Hut on her way through Ennerdale. Years ago, when my dear friend, Brian Wilkinson, was warden at Black Sail, I had spent many happy weekends and holidays climbing and walking the fells there.

Brian had given me a special Black Sail Mug potted by a friend of his at Whitehaven – it is unique and much prized. As a reward for being such an amazing walker, I planned to give it to Rachael so that she could use it for her drinks when she reached Black Sail! Ian was going to carry it for her hidden in his rucksack and produce it 'just like that!'

Although Ian had already taken over 2,500 photos on their two C2C journeys, this time he was also going to make a home movie of memorable and thrilling moments on the way – Rachael proudly posing with her Black Sail mug would, certainly, be one of them!

Coast to Coast Walkers

LOFT BECK, Ennerdale

If you intend to walk up Loft Beck (east of Black Sail YH) as part of your coast to coast walk, only do so if you are an experienced mountaineer. There is snow and ice on the path and a cornice at the very top. Scarth Gap is a good alternative, but again, please take care.

See pictures below taken on 25/3/13

Near top of Loft Beck   At start of Loft Beck   Deep snow on path

Black Sail YH   Cornice at top of loft beck

The poster from Mountain Rescue which meant adding many more miles to our walk!

Nearly beaten by the British Weather

As you would expect, Rachael's C2C 3 2013 was planned by Ian with his usual meticulous attention to detail especially regarding the safety aspects as the start date – Saturday 30th March – was much earlier in the year than two previous C2Cs. This was, as you know, to make sure that Rachael completed her incredible three C2Cs at Robin Hood's Bay on her ninth birthday – 17th April.

However as readers will remember the weather in March 2013 was horrendous – freezing temperatures, unceasing snow and incredibly high winds whipping the deep snow into huge drifts across the regions of the Pennines, Wales and the Lake District in particular. People were cut off for days and the traffic was paralysed – it seemed that no-one was going anywhere!

Ian could plan for most eventualities but, even Ian, could not control the weather. No-one had anticipated that it would be so dreadful and last for so long – the worst conditions for over 24 years. After all, the previous year had temperatures of 21 degrees for the same period!

Walkers were just not walking – the snow was tremendously deep, the wind chill was unbelievably high and paths were icy and dangerous. Guests kept arriving at Old Water View absolutely scared stiff and exhausted – one poor man staggered in having battled his way down from Grisedale Tarn and exclaimed to Ian,

'I really thought that I was going to die! I badly need a drink in your bar before I go to my room, please, perhaps several.'

He stayed there warm, relaxed and safe for quite some time.

Another guest following the same route from Grasmere to Patterdale which in normal conditions is a gentle scenic climb with a breathtaking view of the picturesque Grisedale Tarn nestling below Helvellyn and then a long but easy walk down Grisedale Valley to Patterdale had an awful life-threatening experience!

When he reached the tarn the whole saddle was covered in treacherously deep snow and ice and the path just completely disappeared. He stepped forwards thinking he knew the way and sank into a snowdrift which utterly buried him – he was in way over his head! Fortunately another man following him realised what had happened and was able eventually to dig the poor man out potentially saving his life.

After a brief rest, both men, very sensibly, decided to turn back and descend to Grasmere from where they got a taxi to Old Water View.

Just below the Kirkstone Pass, 18 Red Deer were found frozen to death in a huge impenetrable snowdrift – something that none of the locals ever remember happening before! The severe weather conditions just continued – the cold biting wind and icy snow storms were relentless.

Understandably, Ian was a very concerned dad – he had an unbelievably, enthusiastic 8 year old who was completely oblivious of all the dangers and could not wait to start her C2C 3 – yet he was responsible for her safety and well-being!

He did not want to disappoint Rachael but he was intensely aware of difficulties and additional hazards that the dreadful weather had brought and was really worried – what should he do?

In addition, because of the weather, Ian suddenly had financial problems – he had lost roughly £4,500 income due to cancellations over two weekends at Easter (usually a vital source of income for hotel and B&B owners in The Lakes as they recover from the winter period.) He originally had 48 guests booked in to Old Water View but 45 had to cancel as they were unable make the journey.

Ian had almost impossible decisions to make – but some things in life are more important than money. Somehow he would afford it. Rachael must be given the opportunity to achieve her dream!

One decision made – now the safety aspects. Using his experience of the C2C and the Lakes, Ian was able to modify their route so that most potential dangers could be avoided and he knew that he would be able to protect his precious daughter. They would go!!

Sadly Rachael's beloved Black Sail Hut had to close. It was buried in a snow drift and the snow had blown inside and affected the electricity and other power supplies. So Ian booked them in at the Youth Hostel at Buttermere – a good compromise because this meant that they did not have to cross the impassable Loft Beck trail. However this added an extra seven miles to this C2C – 192 + 7 = 199 miles!

He still planned to carry the Black Sail mug that I was giving her as a surprise but Rachael would be drinking out of it at Ennerdale Bridge instead of Black Sail. She would be just as thrilled – Rachael has such a joyful outlook on life, she can deal with small disappointments and remain completely happy – after all she was walking with her dad.

Just before I drove them to the beginning of their epic journey at St. Bees, fate added yet another little twist – the microwave in Ian's kitchen 'blew up' and his printer refused to print.

Grandma Joyce, like Ian, wasn't the only one who was apprehensive about the next few weeks – what would happen next!!

Rightly so, as readers will soon realise, because even when the snow and ice no longer presented such a threat, the strong bitingly cold wind which blew incessantly throughout their journey brought its own hazards. Rachael and Ian faced a massive, continuous challenge this time around!

'Look Dad! I'm over half a stone block taller than when I started my C2C 1!'

Left: Pebbles to carry for the family all the way to Robin Hood's Bay. **Right:** We are off!

Left: 'Willy' the bear is going to see quite a lot on this trip. Note his Mountain Rescue badge.
Right: Rachael introducing the video of her C2C 3 – watch out Julia Bradbury!

The beginning of Rachael's C2C3

At last the start day, March 30th, of Rachael's C2C 3 dawned. She was incredibly excited – literally jumping up and down in her eagerness to begin. However Daddy and Grandma Joyce had to care for Ian's guests before any last minute packing could be done.

When the last guest had left suitably replete with one of Ian's famous breakfasts, the packing could begin. Understandably most of the clothing was Rachael's as we were very concerned especially because of the on-going harsh weather conditions that she should have the correct gear to help her complete her huge challenge.

Fortunately Rachael has grown a great deal since her last C2C 2 so as I am only five feet tall most of my Himalayan trekking gear fitted her – fleece trousers, liners, base layers, fleece, gilet and a waterproof that had withstood monsoon rainfall in Nepal's high Himalayas. She also had my Everest down jacket and spikes (crampons) as well as her own gear including all of the clothing etc. given to her by the Patterdale Mountain Rescue Team. We were comforted to know that she was as well-equipped as possible to meet any additional problems caused by the dreadful weather. At one point, Rachael did ask, 'Have you got any clothes left, Grandma Joyce?

'Not a lot', was my reply, 'but that is no problem. All I want, Rachael, is for you to be safe and warm.

Also firmly fixed to her rucksack was the little bear mascot, Willy, that I had given her for Christmas. He was going to see some amazing, beautiful and scary sights!

Left: One mile already done! Only 191 miles to go! **Right:** Rachael and friends.

And so we left Old Water View in my little car which just was not fast enough for Rachael – if she could have flown to St. Bees, she would. Even restricted by her seat belt, she was bouncing around in the back seat trying to urge my little car to speed up.

'Can't we go any faster, please, please!' she asked.

We were travelling at the correct speed limit at the time. Then, of course, the 'How long before we get to St. Bees?' began – the first before we even reached Keswick! Rachael could hardly contain her excitement – she was literally bursting with such enthusiasm that we thought she would explode.

As we reached the first St. Bees sign, Ian filmed Rachael pointing to the cliff path that is the start of the Coast to Coast adventure. She is an absolutely natural presenter – watch out Julia Bradbury!

When we reached the car park at St. Bees, Rachael leapt out of the car and ran towards the beach. The tide was in so the waves, driven by a stiff breeze, were lapping at our feet! We duly selected our pebbles, including those for other family members and gave them to Ian who would carry them all the way to Robin Hood's Bay. (That's what Dads are for!)

Then, of course as is the custom, Rachael went to dip her boots in the Irish Sea. In fact she was nearly caught by the waves and had to race back up the beach, giggling loudly, to avoid getting her boots soaked. Ian, who was making a home movie of this C2C 3, caught all this on video.

Next came the obligatory posing for a photograph at Wainwright's monument – we were astonished to note, by the height on one of the stone blocks, just how much Rachael had grown since her first magnificent C2C at the age of seven!

Lots of hugs and wishes of 'Good Luck!' and then, eagerly clutching her well-deserved ice cream, Rachael ran up the path towards the cliffs that lead to the lighthouse with Daddy in pursuit. I must admit that I had a huge lump in my throat as I watched that brave little girl, dressed like a Himalayan explorer, disappear into the distance.

I dropped their luggage off at Stonehouse Farm and set off to drive back to Old Water View to face my own challenge.

Trying again to fill Ian's size 13 shoes with my own, totally inadequate size six's because, of course, when doing the two C2Cs with Rachael and the one with Catherine, Ian did not 'abandon' his beloved Old Water View but entrusted the care of his guests to his wonderful staff and to me.

St. Bees to Ennerdale Bridge.

The weather at St. Bees was utterly bizarre – in spite of the breeze, it was sunny and warm – more like Spain, while in the distance to the east, the high fells of the Lake District were completely covered with snow. They would be walking there in a few days. It had actually snowed a little earlier that morning in Patterdale.

Rachael soon began to shed some of her layers of clothing as she was really hot but undeterred she climbed gaily up to the top of the cliffs and skipped along the path to the lighthouse where yet again they turned their faces east towards Robin Hood's Bay over 190 miles away.

It was on this cliff path that Rachael asked Ian if they could begin an impromptu challenge,

'Daddy don't you think it would be a good idea to have another sort of challenge besides the Tractor One you've planned. Because phone boxes are so important in case of emergency, we could conduct a scientific survey of how many phone boxes can be seen on the C2C?'

Clever Rachael realised that if there were two challenges, she had more chance of winning at least one – two would obviously be better!

In place of last year's Post Van Challenge, which you may remember was won by Catherine; Ian had invented a new Daily Challenge for Rachael and himself – 'The Tractor Challenge.' 'A competition to see who could spot the most tractors – one point for a blue, yellow or green tractor but two points for a red one and a bonus point for one with a flashing light on top!'

Snow-capped Lakeland peaks in the distance.

At the end – Robin Hood's Bay – Ian decided that the daily tally would be added up and the loser would buy the winner a large ice cream of their choice.

Ian was absolutely determined to win – even if he had to cheat somehow. (He knew that Rachael would if she could.) However there was the penalty of deducting a point if caught cheating.

Ian doesn't learn, does he? With a confident voice he announced that he had seen two tractors with flashing orange lights round the next corner. He was the winner for the day because Rachael had only seen 1 tractor on the way into St. Bees. His triumph was definitely short-lived as when they rounded the corner, his mysterious tractors had disappeared.

'Wow! Daddy, you were cheating!' exclaimed Rachael. 'Now you are two points behind me because I did see a real tractor and you've just lost a point because you made yours up!'

Ian's humiliation continued because Rachael soon spotted a barn in which there were nine tractors. She was ecstatic,

'See – I am the true winner, Daddy – I am 11 points in front of you!'

Sadly for Ian, this was to be the pattern for the next 17 days – serves him right, doesn't it?

Ian had planned a short first day for them so they returned to Stonehouse Farm via the pretty path near to the railway line – a route unknown to Rachael. For the first time ever, Rachael had a small blister apparently caused by Grandma Joyce's woollen socks!

After a pleasant meal in the Queen's Head they were treated to a fabulous

The old fashioned way to 'log-in!'.

sunset over the sparkling Irish Sea. It was breathtaking – every shade of gold, orange, red and purple filling the darkening sky. As they wheeled and dived overhead in a noisy chorus, the seagulls seemed to be greeting Rachael and wishing her 'Good Luck' for her incredible challenge!

Next morning, having had an hour's less sleep due to the clocks going forwards, they set off towards the snow-covered mountains to re-join Wainwright's path. It was so warm and sunny that they were walking in T-shirts. Unlike yesterday there were no horses, lambs or chickens to be seen but lots of dogs being walked by a variety of owners.

Sadly the lovely lanes were completely spoilt by lots of ugly litter in the hedgerows and on the grass verges. Someone surely should make certain that this is cleared up – thousands of visitors from all over the world take up Wainwright's challenging walk every year and this mess is a sad reflection of this part of the beautiful Lake District.

To vary the route from the previous years, Ian decided that they wouldn't climb Dent hill again but instead walk the picturesque path around the bottom and then join the Nannycatch Valley at Nannycatch Gate. This was the last place, where looking backwards to the west, they could still catch a glimpse of the Irish Sea. Rachael was completely enthralled by this pretty secret valley and skipped along completely absorbed by the scenery until they reached the Shepherds Arms at Ennerdale Bridge.

She spent the remainder of the afternoon playing happily like any child on the swings in the park, her blister entirely forgotten. She had spotted seven phone boxes already – four today and three yesterday.

Drinking from my special Black Sail mug.

This day was Easter Sunday. A long time before Rachael began her C2C 3, she had asked Ian if there really was an Easter Bunny. As always, when asked about such things like the Tooth Fairy or indeed Santa Claus, Ian had replied,

'If you really believe in the Easter Bunny, then it is true.'

So Rachael had written a letter to the Easter Bunny asking for an Easter egg to be delivered to Black Sail on Easter Monday. Now, of course, the next venue was changed to Buttermere Youth Hostel instead of Black Sail. Rachael was very concerned,

'But I really, really want an Easter egg at Easter, Daddy, but the Easter Bunny thinks I am at Black Sail so she'll take it there!'

Ian, you will remember, was carrying an Easter egg for Rachael with my Black Sail mug so he answered somewhat smugly,

'Don't worry, darling, write another letter to the Easter Bunny and she is very clever – she will deliver your egg to Buttermere instead. I'm sure she will.'

'Okay!' replied Rachael and cheerfully began to compose her letter.

What do they say about 'the best laid plans of mice and men' – everything was going well until Ian decided that he ought to give Rachael my present – my Black Sail mug here at Ennerdale Bridge as it is the nearest point they would be to the Ennerdale Valley and the path up to Black Sail. She was overjoyed and unbelievably proud of her unique mug and immediately had a drink in it carefully holding the mug by the body and not relying on the handle.

Unfortunately Ian neglected to close his rucksack properly so Rachael found the hidden Easter egg!

'Daddy!' she exclaimed accusingly, 'You were carrying that Easter egg for me, weren't you but that is from you and I want one from the Easter Bunny too. Please, please!'

'You'll have to wait and see,' replied Ian, privately thinking, 'How do I get out of this one?'

For once he did not have a cunning plan – clearly he needed a miracle!

Ennerdale Bridge to Buttermere Youth Hostel

Beautiful sunshine greeted them the next morning as they set off on their long walk to Buttermere – a day which due to the necessary diversion was seven miles longer than originally planned.

As they left the Shepherds Arms, they noticed a large poster put up by the Mountain Rescue Service which really highlighted the still dangerous conditions on the high fells. There were photos of Black Sail Hut almost buried in the snow and Loft Beck just above Black Sail completely blocked. The poster warned walkers not to attempt the climb as the conditions were extremely hazardous with snow drifts, ice and hanging cornices! A different world from where they were but, amazingly, only a few miles away.

Rachael laughed with delight as she pointed to a house they were passing – obviously 'The Cat House' as it had a cat sitting in every window and each one looking at them with the superior look that cats have perfected over the years.

As they continued towards Loweswater, a man in a white van drew up beside them. Apparently he was the support driver for family friends doing the St. Beda's Walk which follows a similar route in this area. He was carrying Easter Cup Cakes especially for the children – lovely little cakes topped with small multi-coloured Easter eggs which he was delivering to them at Ennerdale Bridge.

He had several spare cakes and was genuinely pleased when he recognised Rachael from the pub the previous evening, so he duly gave her an Easter Cup Cake and wished her every success and a very Happy Easter!

Excitedly Rachael thanked the man and with a 'Wow!' she just bounced on ahead – as Ian said, 'It was just as if she was walking on air.'

'This is yummy! Delicious!' she cried munching happily, 'You see, Daddy, this is how the Easter Bunny does things but that man didn't look much like an Easter Bunny, did he?'

'He probably works for the Easter Bunny,' Ian explained. How lucky was that! Ian had his miracle – and a thoroughly elated and satisfied little walker.

When they first caught sight of lovely Loweswater, Ian urged Rachael to sit on a gate so he could interview her with the fantastic background of the

Left: Happy Easter! **Right:** A Cumbrian road sign – in the snow and the sun!

Stunning Crummock Water.

shimmering water and the snowy fells behind her. As she tried to climb down, she got caught up on the gate and fell off in a heap – Whoops! She looked so funny that they both had a fit of giggles.

And so on to enchanting Crummock Water, probably one of the most picturesque of the lakes. The scenery was breathtaking – the sun was shining on the glittering water and the high snowy fells were mirrored on its still surface. Both Rachael and Ian stood there silently in wonderment – they were absolutely entranced. It was one of those magical moments that live in your memories forever!

To add to the enchantment three buzzards circled lazily high above in the clear blue sky.

In spite of the seemingly endless miles, Rachael said that this was the best day's walk of her life and her favourite view of all the views she had seen on her C2Cs.

'What a marvellous, amazing day, Daddy!' she murmured blissfully, ' I might not have a big Easter Egg but I had something far better – a yummy Easter Cup Cake with lots of little eggs on it brought by a random man in a white van. My blister has gone and I'm so glad that Black Sail was closed because I will be able to go back there with you another day!'

Rachael certainly sees the positive side of all situations.

Ian, too, preferred this day to the walk up Ennerdale so much so that he decided they would come back and stay a few days in the area so they could explore the fells together.

The hostel at Buttermere proved to be a great success too – alright it was not our beloved Black Sail but it was a really friendly pleasant place with good food and a warm welcome. They would certainly return there one day soon.

Buttermere to Rosthwaite

It was really very cold and windy when they left the Youth Hostel next morning and walked down to the lake edge and through a tunnel intending to follow the interesting lakeside path. They were about halfway along when Ian realised that his mobile phone was not in his pocket and he didn't know where it was. As the weather was much harsher and would be increasingly so as they climbed higher, a mobile phone was a necessity so they turned back to the hostel. After searching for some time, Ian found his mobile in the pocket of the trousers which he had put in the dirty laundry bag in their luggage awaiting transport – lucky man – they would be safe again.

When Ian opened his rucksack to take out his gloves, an apple escaped and bounced down to the lakeside with Rachael chasing it.

Left: The tunnel beside Buttermere.   **Right:** It's very cold and a long way to the top of Honister Pass.

Left: On the way down to Rosthwaite.   **Right:** Meet 'Pip' the Parrot.

A beautiful Borrowdale morning.

'Daddy, I've got it!' she shouted triumphantly holding the offending apple high, 'I've caught it just like I did for Catherine last year but it is a bit dented!'

Next came the long steep road climb up to the summit of the Honister Pass. Fortunately there was very little traffic. By now they were surrounded by snow and the wind was bitingly cold. The beck which normally tumbles in a cascade of bubbling water down to the valley bottom was completely frozen over.

They were in an entirely different world from the last two days. At last they reached the top of the pass and paused to gaze at the magnificent panoramic view that opened up before them – snow covered fells around them and white glistening high mountains in the distance with spectacular green patches of grass peeping through the snowy banks and rocks.

It was too cold to linger so they had lunch in the café at Honister Quarry. Ian thought it was a good idea to point out to the lady who served them, that there was water running through the fluorescent light fitting near them – she was horrified! Thankfully there were no immediate fireworks but, nevertheless, they ate quickly and were soon on their way down the snow-covered but easy packhorse trail to Rosthwaite.

When they arrived at Gillercombe – their B&B, Rachael had two unexpected surprises – the owner's name was Rachel and she had a very friendly African grey parrot called Pip. Rachael soon had it perching on her shoulder!

In her journal she wrote, 'The view from my bed is amazing. There is a massive window and the view through it is absolutely stunning – I can see everything – what a great place! And I saw three more phone boxes today.'

They had dinner at the Langstrath Hotel and went to sleep quite early – it had been quite a hard, cold day but to Rachael it had seemed easy!

Rosthwaite to Keswick and then Grasmere

Their next destination was Grasmere and normally to get there, they would have climbed up Greenup Edge and down Far Easedale Valley but the snow drifts were so deep on this route, as Rachael observed, they were even higher than Daddy (and would certainly have buried Rachael and Grandma Joyce) so a safe route via Keswick was necessary.

They walked along the Cumbria Way, a beautiful riverside walk and a path around superb scenic Derwentwater where Rachael posed by two giant wooden hands. Ian also took a photo of an acrobatic sheep which, much to Rachael's amusement kept jumping up and standing on its hind legs so it could eat from a tree!

From Keswick, they caught a bus to Grasmere – sadly it was not the open air bus that Ian had hoped was running but Rachael cheerfully accepted this and commented on the lovely scenery she could see through the bus windows. That evening she wrote in her journal,

'We walked the correct number of miles today but because of safety we ended up in the wrong place and it was so hot that I got a bit of sunburn because I did not wear my sunhat. Four more phone boxes to add to the total.'

The weather conditions and temperatures on the high fells and those down in the valleys are so unbelievably different that even experienced and well-equipped walkers can be caught out.

Grasmere to Patterdale

Rachael and Ian left Chestnut Villa, their overnight B&B in Grasmere in bright sunshine. They spent a relaxed half hour watching a helicopter carrying bags of boulders to repair the eroded paths on the surrounding fells. The walking conditions were idyllic, warm sunshine and a gentle breeze until they climbed up to the snowline some three miles from Grasmere. Ian was able to take lots of photos and interview Rachael – she is a real little star and loves performing for the camera.

'In safe hands' – the path alongside Derwentwater.

Home tomorrow!

Left: This is the part that Rachael had been waiting for – a walk above the snowline. **Right:** Foot Spikes on – let's go!

But now the serious and potentially hazardous part of the day's walk began. Ian made sure that Rachael was correctly kitted up with in all her warm, windproof clothing and had her walking pole and sunglasses to protect her eyes from the glare of the sun on the snow. They were both wearing spikes on their boots.

Initially Ian took some really dramatic shots of Rachael bouncing up and down in the snow and videoed her tackling the steep snow slopes with determination and laughter. As the ground grew even steeper, he put the video camera in his pocket. This was the time to concentrate completely on the conditions underfoot and ahead. In such terrain, absolute, meticulous observation and previous knowledge are vital to ensure safety. As they approached the saddle between Helvellyn and Fairfield, Ian was dismayed to see that it was still impossible to distinguish between the path and the margins of Grisedale Tarn. Everywhere there were snowdrifts and ice and no footprints to show where others had gone.

Ian held Rachael's hands tightly and with a confident, calm, reassuring and loving voice guided her every step. What Ian did not know until later, was that the video camera was still switched on and was taking unusual footage of the mesh lining of his pocket! But more importantly it recorded all his comforting words to Rachael and, bless her, it also recorded her trusting and brave responses. Clearly by the tone of her voice you could tell that she was scared but had implicit faith in her Daddy.

Slowly, patiently and skilfully, Ian guided her around what he judged were the margins of the entirely frozen tarn – one step at a time. Frequently, they could see the water under the ice and down through it to the treacherous icy and snowy boulders beneath.

Reaching the summit near Grisedale.

Left: Grisedale Tarn frozen over! **Right:** Icicles bigger than my Dad!

Rachael's pole kept getting stuck and the ice was incredibly slippery but their spikes were really effective. Their progress was painfully slow but Ian was determined and experienced enough to keep his precious daughter safe.

(When they were back at Old Water View, Ian admitted to me that at this point he had felt that he was at the very edge of his ability and resources – the responsibility was enormous and would continue to be so, all the way to Robin Hood's Bay.)

They were both concentrating so hard that neither of them noticed that Rachael's scarf had slipped down her face leaving her right cheek exposed. This was to cause her problems days later when she developed a cold.

Snow-covered Fairfield.

Gradually Rachael grew more confident as they descended to more stable, safer ground where they did not have to watch every step and so were able to look around a little. Rachael was amazed at the size of the huge shining icicles hanging off Eagle Crag – they were bigger than Daddy!

The views were spectacular – huge mountain ridges covered with glistening snow and ice, patches of green beginning to appear between the rocks and in the distance the sparkle of the stream released from its icy prison tumbling down the valley with yet more shimmering, snowy fells ahead and a glimpse of gleaming Ullswater.

About halfway down between Grisedale Tarn and Ruthwaite Lodge, a climbing hut, Ian was astonished and shocked to see some 20 teenagers approaching them dressed in T shirts, jeans and trainers – totally inappropriate clothing for the Fells even when the weather is good and probably lethal in the conditions that Rachael and Ian had just experienced.

Bragging and laughing, they told Ian that they were going to climb Dollywagon Pike, go over Helvellyn and then cross the Dodds and descend via Sticks Pass to Glenridding. This is a long, difficult route in good weather for seasoned walkers and would be very dangerous for these teenagers. Ian told them that they should turn round because what they planned to do was impossible with all the snow and ice above the snowline – they would need warm clothing and spikes – but they completely ignored his advice and raced ahead.

The Cockpit Stone Circle – Askham Fell.

When Ian turned round again, he saw that they were sword-fighting using the icicles from Eagle Crag!

Rachael, who of course, has been brought up in the Lakes and understands the dangers of the Fells and thoroughly respects the mountains, was scathing about the behaviour of the teenagers,

'Are they mad, Daddy?' she asked,' Or are they are just stupid and is no-one guiding them?'

A good question that was answered about five minutes later when a man in an ordinary anorak, T-shirt, jeans and no spikes asked Ian if he had seen some school kids! Apparently this was the teacher who was responsible for the teenagers. Unbelievable! They were breaking every law of the mountains and Ian feared for the lives of them all. Hastily he begged the man to try to catch up with his charges, stop them from trying to climb further and bring them down safely. The man had little hope of succeeding as the teenagers were so far ahead and obviously were not going to listen to anyone!

Ian could do no more and he had Rachael to care for – she was his priority for although emotionally she was still very excited and thrilled to be walking with Daddy, she was physically drained – the cold had really affected her and although spikes were no longer needed, her steps were still a little laboured and unsteady. However our brave, resilient Rachael is never down for long – a rest and lunch sitting outside Ruthwaite Lodge and she became more like her bouncy, happy self as they both trekked down Grisedale Valley to

Looking back towards Patterdale and the last of the snow (for now!).

Patterdale and home – Old Water View which was bathed in winter sunshine in the valley bottom.

In spite of a rough day, Rachael was ecstatic and triumphant – she had conquered all of her fears and overcome all difficulties and she absolutely fine – it was just great to be home and she had experienced her first snow hike!

(Ian heard no more about the teenagers and their 'teacher' and the Mountain Rescue Team were not called out so it looks as though they escaped without injuries – they were very lucky!)

Next day was a rest day at Old Water View, at least for Rachael but not for Ian or Grandma Joyce! Ian, ever versatile, changed from his walking gear and donned his smart Old Water View Uniform and we prepared for the wedding of Eileen and Ian Faill.

Old Water View is an ideal venue for a small wedding – the location is fabulous and all the rooms are occupied by the bride and groom's guests. Ian closes to the public while the wedding party is there so they have the venue completely to themselves including the bar and the services of the award-winning chef who provides a varied and comprehensive menu to order.

The bride and groom were utterly thrilled and so were all their guests,

'Thank you for a fabulous wedding. It is exactly what we wanted!' Ian and Eileen told us, 'It could not have been better. We have all had a marvellous time!' So had we!

Now Ian had all his gear and Rachael's to sort out for the next morning when they were walking to Bampton. Ian had decided because of the ice, snow and high winds on the Fells not to attempt the climb up to The Knott and Kidsty Pike and the high route to Bampton but to follow Wainwright's alternative winter route – the picturesque path through Howtown and up over Askham Fell and then a walk along the pretty lanes to their 'comfy' B&B – Bampton Village Store and Post Office.

For this part of their adventure, they were joined by Ian and Jackie and their friendly black Labrador, Jack. He certainly kept Rachael amused and although very clearly her cold was developing, she marched on cheerfully in the sunshine simply glad to be walking with friends and Daddy again in the beautiful countryside.

As she remarked later, 'All your friends are nice, Daddy and Jack is a lovely dog. What a great day!'

Although this route is not as spectacular as the path over Kidsty Pike, the views looking back towards Ullswater are fabulous and particularly this time as mighty Helvellyn, Fairfield and all the surrounding fells were completely covered in snow and shining like huge beacons among the fluffy white clouds scudding across the blue sky. Ian's friends remarked that they had recently been trekking in Peru but had not seen anything that matched the awesome beauty of the scene before them. Rachael was simply entranced.

It was only when we read Rachael's journal that we realised although she had walked and skipped with her usual enthusiasm, she hadn't been well at all that day. She wrote…

'It was an easy walk today but I felt poorly! I saw one phone box.'

Bampton to Orton

The weather was sunny as Rachael and Ian set out for Orton the next day but the wind was bitterly cold – the kind that 'takes your breath away.'

The first four miles into Shap, Rachael found easy and she spent some happy moments standing on the M6 motorway bridge waving to the truck drivers who responded by bleeping at her. Then she discovered that she had lost the back off one of her earrings,

'Oh, dear!' she exclaimed, 'Daddy, it must have dropped on the back of one of those trucks so either it's on its way south to London or north to Scotland!'

A quick phone call to Grandma Joyce and a replacement was sent to Orton via Sherpa.

They had lunch in as sheltered position as they could find on the limestone plateau – Rachael describes this, 'We had to have lunch outside because we could not find the café.'

Left: Bye, bye Lake District! **Right:** Who will win the tractor challenge?

The amazing Limestone plateau – a welcome lull in the wind and brief warm sunshine!

(There wasn't one – this is an example of a Rachael joke – she has a similar weird sense of humour as Ian!)

However as the high, open limestone plateau is very exposed and extremely windy. Soon poor Rachael began to struggle – walking against the wind is very tiring and clearly her cold was getting worse so she had problems breathing. Ian became increasingly concerned for her as he could plainly see that his little girl was rapidly becoming drained of energy. He asked her frequently if she wanted to stop but Rachael, as always, bravely insisted that she wanted to carry on walking and putting her head down, she battled ahead – her determination and sense of humour keeping her going.

She observed, 'Dad plotted a whole new route and didn't look at a map and we didn't get lost! Wow!'

About a mile away from Orton, Ian took another small diversion across some fields and they were both surprised to see a man fast asleep in the grass – he had no rucksack or other walking gear but was just stretched out on his back with a Stetson-like hat over his face.

Apart from a few giggles, they walked past him quietly but they must have disturbed him, because when Ian looked round, the man was following them.

'Look, Rachael, there's a bear following us!' exclaimed Ian – and, indeed, the man was really hairy and looked like a bear.

'Don't be silly, Daddy!' answered Rachael with a toss of her head, 'It's that man who was asleep.'

'Oh no, it isn't', insisted Ian – 'It's a bear and it's going to overtake you and beat you to Orton!'

'Never!' was Rachael's reply and marched on with renewed vigour and determination and triumphantly reached Orton first – bear or man, she'd beaten him! Although obviously not at her best, Rachael was still unbelievably competitive. Ian did have a secret smile on his face – clever Daddy!

The lady behind the counter at the George Hotel recognised Rachael from photos and articles in the local press and gave her a huge welcome,

'You're famous, Rachael, well done!' she said.

Ian, in turn, also recognised the lady but was puzzled as to where he had met her – certainly not as a guest at Old Water View. Then he remembered – she used to have a small shop and café at a Trout Farm where Ian used to deliver his jam – small world isn't it?

Although Rachael had 'perked up' somewhat, her cold was getting worse so there wasn't a single protest when Ian suggested that they went to bed early. Hopefully a good night's sleep would help her.

Orton to Kirkby Stephen

Before they left the George Hotel for Kirkby Stephen, Rachael confessed that she really felt poorly that morning and didn't even seem very bothered about selecting some chocolate from the Chocolate Factory – that is totally unlike her.

Obviously Ian asked her again if she wanted to stop but Rachael would not admit defeat – tenacious as ever, she battled on stubbornly but, unusually for her, she kept asking Ian for frequent rests.

Ian realised that Rachael was becoming increasingly exhausted and tragically near the end of her ability. He knew that this was not going to get better and was really worried about the situation – keeping his precious daughter safe was his priority now.

It was absolutely freezing – the icy wind grew stronger and they could both feel and see the tiny particles of ice that were battering against them. Rachael was wearing all of her warm, wind and waterproof clothes with scarves covering her face like a mask, but she was still shivering. When, at last, they reached Sunbiggin Tarn, Rachael collapsed at the foot of a wall unable to walk any further.

'I can't do it, Daddy! I really can't do it' she cried, utterly distraught.

It was heart-breaking to hear her admit that and to see that state she was in. Ian was devastated – it was obvious that Rachael could not carry on so he made the difficult but sensible decision that for this year, their C2C was over. They were going home now – but how?

Although they were in a fairly isolated spot, Ian was well aware that they were not too far from help if only they could reach it. He realised that Rachael was too heavy for him to carry any distance but Ian also knew that he had to get her up and walking or she would succumb to hypothermia.

This is the situation that all parents dread, when you have 'to be cruel to be kind.' Ian shouted loudly at Rachael and forced her up onto her feet and holding both of her hands tightly and with many urges of 'Come on, Rachael!' he managed to walk her to the nearest road which thankfully was only a few hundred yards away hidden in a fold of the hills.

Luckily, he was soon able to flag down a kind lady in a car who, seeing Rachael's obvious distress, gave them a lift to a café and garden centre about two miles off their route. Here Rachael would be warm and comparatively safe for a while.

Ian quickly bought Rachael some hot blackcurrant juice, gave her some medication and leaving her with her drink, he tried to make arrangements for a taxi to take them home. When he turned around, Rachael was stretched across the table fast asleep. Half an hour or so later, she woke up and Ian explained about the taxi.

'Please, Daddy, I'm feeling much better now, so please, please I don't want to stop. Can we go on to our B&B in Kirkby Stephen and decide in the morning whether or not we should go home? I really, really want to try and carry on, please!' she pleaded.

This seemed like a sensible suggestion and clearly she had 'bounced back' mentally at least. Knowing how much this C2C meant to Rachael, Ian agreed to delay the decision until the next morning. Fortunately the lady with the car was going to Kirkby Stephen so she gladly gave them a lift. Ian bought some more medication for Rachael and their B&B, Fletcher House, was open, so after giving her a drink and medicine, he put Rachael to bed and she slept soundly all that afternoon.

In the evening Rachael got up for a meal at their usual pub but, sadly, unlike previous years, she was too tired to play in the sand pit. They returned to

Left: Feeling poorly and cold but not wanting to stop. **Right:** Approaching Sunbiggin Tarn and feeling really poorly!

Looking back at the footage of their walk and working out how to persuade Dad to let her go on!

Fletcher House and Rachael went back to bed quickly and slept all through the night without waking up. As he watched her sleeping peacefully, Ian felt completely humbled and incredibly proud of his amazingly courageous little girl – what would tomorrow bring, he wondered. He was almost in tears as he read her journal for the day,

'The weather today was very cold and very windy so I was feeling really ill – most of the way I felt dizzy and sick and my head hurt so much that I could not see or walk properly. I felt so ill I honestly thought that I was not going to finish the C2C 3 … … a kind lady gave us a lift … … I slept all afternoon … … I feel a bit better and hope we can carry on tomorrow!'

Even though she had been very ill, her mind was completely focussed on trying to complete this C2C.

Kirkby Stephen to Keld

Joy! Next morning, Rachael really looked much better – her cold had dried-up and she was bright-eyed and ready for a challenge.

'Can we walk to Keld today, please Daddy?' she asked 'I know I can do it and I love that walk and we can come back another day and walk the miles I missed yesterday.'

Rachael was very concerned about doing the 'correct' mileage! Ian pointed out that because of the necessary diversions they had already done, she had walked about ten extra miles already, so the few miles lost yesterday did not matter. This seemed to satisfy Rachael as she didn't mention it again.

As she skipped joyfully ahead, admiring the scenery and pointing out unusual cloud shapes and the sparkling snow on the trees, walls and grass verges, Ian knew that now they would finish this C2C 3 – he had his happy, wonderful little walker back – what a lucky dad, he was!

It was a wonderful day in so many ways – above all Rachael had bounced back, there were just a few short flurries of snow and the bitter wind had dropped a little. The snowy scenery was spectacular – gleaming snow-capped hills, huge wind-driven snow drifts and trees and hedgerows garlanded in luminous white lacy raiment.

Shortly, as last year, Rachael paused briefly to have a swing on a tyre, but then swiftly strode ahead obviously feeling that she had to prove that she really was better and making up for yesterday.

The snow on the grass verges was very deep in places, up to six foot, so inevitably, Rachael, decided to leave her footprints there, lots of fun and giggles in the snow!

A little further on, the snow was even higher – covering a C2C signpost to within three inches of the top – higher than Rachael!

Ian was able to point out lots of birds new to her including curlews, lapwings and oyster catchers. In fact when they spotted an oyster catcher in a nearby field, they decided to see how close they could get to it – they crept silently behind a long low wall peering over it now and again – just like a pair of SAS soldiers on a mission. They managed to get within a few yards of it before it flew away so Rachael was able to store its vivid image in her memory.

Not at one point did Rachael ask for a rest and would not stop even to eat her lunch. When they reached that really steep hill that is marked by posts, Ian thought that she must slow down. No! Not Rachael! Exuberantly, she literally sprinted to the top and stood there arms uplifted like the triumphant winner she is. Marvelling at her sheer guts and determination, Ian, with a proud smile on his face, followed her to their destination for the day – Keld Lodge – the halfway point of the C2C.

Left: Back to full fitness and 'full of beans' – let's go to Keld! **Right:** Snow again!

Left: Rachael had never seen snow this deep before! **Right:** Loving it!

Left: Now that IS deep! A 2m sign post almost completely buried. **Right:** Note the black clouds overhead.

In her notes, Rachael recorded proudly, 'I did not have ONE rest today and I was a lot better. We got to Keld about lunchtime. I saw two phone boxes.'

Keld to Danby Whiske

Rachael woke up early next morning – lively and eager to begin the walk to Reeth but first she had a full cooked breakfast – she certainly had 'bounced back 'and was her usual bright, cheerful self, an absolute joy to be with.

The sky was a little overcast and cloudy so it was cold and misty down on the path by the River Swale but Rachael was obviously just so thrilled to be able to walk as normal that she laughed and skipped joyfully – just full of excitement and wonder. Incredibly, as Rachael recorded, they had not had any rain since they left St. Bees!

About halfway along when they stopped for a snack, they spotted a very strange creature in the river – Rachael described it very well in her journal – 'It was an octopus-like creature – it had a salmon pink body and tentacles about 30cm long and Daddy says it is definitely not a crayfish. It is a mystery.' As yet, in spite of investigations, it remains unidentified – perhaps readers can help?

Behind Rachael and Ian were two C2C ladies with a dog called Harry. They admitted to Ian that they were following him as they did not have a map – why no map or guide, one wonders? After a while Ian realised that the ladies were no longer in sight. They seemed to disappear when Rachael paused on a nearby bridge for a photo and as neither he nor Rachael ever saw them again – where they ended up no-one knows!

When Rachael and Ian reached the pub at Gunnerside they were dismayed to find that it had closed down and that Sid that friendly, greedy cat who had been such a favourite was nowhere to be seen. So they had to sit down outside the empty pub and eat their own sandwiches. Sadly this was the third pub that they had passed so far on the C2C 3 that had closed – the two others being the Mardale Inn at Bampton and The Greyhound Hotel at Shap. (Both have since re-opened.)

They plodded happily on to Reeth where their lovely hosts at their 'fab' B&B – Springfield House were absolutely delighted to see Rachael again. In fact, the lady had a large Easter Bunny with a stack of Easter Eggs that she has been saving for Rachael.

'Wow!' exclaimed Rachael,' The Easter Bunny really does keep her promises, doesn't she Daddy?'

As Rachael wrote later, 'I love this B&B because the owners are lovely people and they have a frog pond in the garden.'

Leaving Keld for the third time.

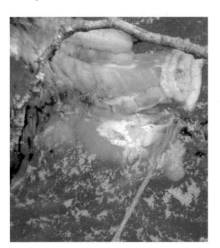

Left: The mysterious creature in the River Swale – Can you tell us, please, what it is? **Right:** Dad tried to claim this one in the tractor challenge!

She quickly went to inspect the pond to see if there were lots of frogs like last year. Unfortunately although there had been lots of frogspawn, the lady owner told Rachael that the naughty cat next door had eaten most of them, as cats will – so only a few frogs this year.

Later Ian and Rachael walked down to the Buck Inn for another well-deserved pizza – Rachael really was back to full bounce!

Left: Reeth – 86 miles to go! **Right:** Rachael had a little lamb!

Reeth to Richmond

It was a warm, sunny day as they set out for Richmond – still windy but not the cold, biting wind they had experienced earlier. They walked up the road and climbed the 101 steps past Marrick Priory, Rachael rushing past Ian to beat him to the top so she could wait for him. Then they followed the same route as previous years to the path under the spectacular Applegarth Scar. When they reached the ancient monument that Catherine had 'broken' last year (well, as Rachael admitted, Catherine had really only dislodged one stone) – Rachael, ever the video-star, did an amusing piece to camera! She was careful not to touch anything so no embarrassing moments this time!

At this point, Ian decided to change the route and follow the Swale into Richmond but soon realised that Wainwright's route was far better for this river walk, although very pretty, involved using a few busy roads.

Then off they marched to their B&B – Old Brewery Guest House which is owned by Sherpa – but where was it? For once, Ian, that well-organised, meticulous man had to ring me up to find its location – well, even Ian, can't be perfect all the time! Later they met up with 'dad's crazy friend Steph' who was to walk with them for the next four days. (Ian has known Steph for some years from when she walked the Pennine Way section of Ian's Land's End to John O'Groats trek.)

They all went for dinner in a rather unpleasant, 'tacky' pub where the tables were sticky and the food not too good either. Rachael, full of beans, was very disappointed and cross when Ian would not let her join in the disco and karaoke – she wanted to sing and dance the night away!

Ian was not being a 'spoilsport'; he was very mindful of just how ill Rachael had been quite recently and knew how much she needed to conserve her energy for the remainder of their journey.

On to Danby Whiske, Ingleby Arncliffe and through to Clay Bank Top

The following morning didn't start too well! Ian and Rachael were up early and organised. They had put their bags on the Sherpa van ready to be transported to their next B&B but Steph had said that she wanted her bags taking too! Now Steph is not the most organised of people so after they had all waited for over an hour and Steph had not turned up – the Sherpa van driver – kind man – went to look for her and found her in Boots Pharmacy with lots of carrier bags which she hoped he could take. No! However, obligingly, he stuffed everything into a large black bin liner and put her name on it. What service – he deserved a medal!

At last they were all ready to carry on to Danby Whiske. Traditionally, whenever they leave Richmond, they always have an ice cream for breakfast (strange custom) and so they began their walk across the Vale of Mowbray clutching their ice creams.

Most C2Coasters say they dislike this part as they think it is boring. Yes, it is different but it has a gentle varied beauty all of its own. For instance if you walk in summer, everything is green and lush with fields, hedgerows and trees bursting with life or in early autumn when the golden corn fields have blood red poppies scattered within their shining, breeze-blown waves. It can be a wonderful journey. But this year as it was really early and the weather had been so dreadful, even Ian who, like Rachael, looks for beauty everywhere, had to admit that the landscape did look very drab, uninteresting and lifeless.

As Rachael remarked, 'It is not as pretty this year.'

However the journey was enlivened by Rachael and Steph who simply 'had a ball' – they just giggled and laughed all the way at the silliest things while Ian listened amused – no wonder Rachael calls her 'Crazy Steph' he thought.

They walked on under the busy A1 road and into Bolton-on-Swale. Rachael was fascinated by the memorial stone to a man called Henry Jenkins was reputedly died at the age of 169 years old.

('I don't think I believe that!' Rachael had written in her journal.')

At last they reached Jean and Brian's home and their B&B, Springfield House at Danby Whiske. Brian was away so, again, not wishing to break with

Left: It has become a tradition to leave Richmond eating an icecream. **Right:** Just a little mud!

Left: 'Willy' seems to be enjoying his adventure too! **Right:** Jean – our host – at Danby Whiske.

tradition, they took Jean to the nearby 'White Swan' for a beer and had one themselves while Rachael had her customary hot chocolate.

Undeservedly, the White Swan has had a bad press due to it being closed when both Wainwright and Julia Bradbury stopped there. But Ian has been there six times on his C2C journeys and Rachael three times and each time they have had really good food there – in fact this time they all thought that it was the best meal they had ever had in a pub on the C2C.

It is always great to start the day with a good laugh – and this happened next morning when they passed an amusing sign on a gate which said – 'No guard dogs – the cat ate them!' (Clearly someone else owns a cat like mine.) Again fits of giggles as they journeyed joyfully on towards Ingleby Arncliffe.

Gerry gets a well-earned break.

The walking was easy over the comparatively flat ground and eventually they climbed over the stile that had the skull, owls and rats attached to the top. As it was early for C2Coasters, the unwelcoming farmer had not yet added any more gruesome trophies.

Unbelievably Ian lost his way when they were crossing an empty, ploughed field – he didn't recognise anything. The terrain was completely different at this time of the year – no paths through the crops or indeed any footprints to show where others had gone. A little shame-faced he had to consult his map and quickly found the correct direction. Next they crossed the busy A19 and Rachael's dreaded railway lines and arrived at their B&B – the Blue Bell Inn without any further incidents.

A little later they went to see their friends Ruth and Gerry. Sadly since last year, their lovely blind dog, Leader, had died. Rachael soon cheered up when they went to the fabulous Ingleby Arncliffe Play Park. This wonderful park was opened in 2010 in memory of 16 year old Andrew Phillips, a local school boy who had lived in the village and campaigned tirelessly for a safe place where the children could play. He had died of a rare form of cancer but his spirit lives on in this remarkable play park.

All the villagers, including Gerry, helped to build it and create the fantastic features many of which were designed by the children. There are dens, a secret garden, lots of climbing frames, a huge zip wire and many other exciting things including the Logs Ness Monster! Rachael, Steph and Gerry 'had an absolute ball' playing there and trying everything out!

Ruth and Gerry – when you read this book, Rachael, Catherine and Ian want you to know how very much your kindness and friendship enhanced all of their C2C's. You really gave them wonderful endings to perfect days.

A windy summit with Roseberry Topping in the background.

Next day although it was reasonably sunny and clear at first, the wind was really strong and quite cold. They climbed up through the pretty woods to the wide open heather moors of Carlton Bank and walked along the paved footpath of the Lyke Wake Walk and Cleveland Way buffeted by huge gusts of wind. Whenever there was a lull, Rachael pointed out lots of interesting landmarks to Steph from this wonderful panoramic stretch of the C2C. In the distance, of course, there is Roseberry Topping – that well-known spectacular mini Matterhorn. Ian decided that later this year, he would definitely invent a pudding deserving of such a name to serve in his restaurant at Old Water View.

Part of the moor here still looks rather like a lunar landscape as the heather has been cleared for the runways for a Gliding Club – an ideal spot for this sport. They all descended carefully towards the place where the unusual Lord's Stone Café used to be sited under a bank and were delighted to see that it was being rebuilt. This news will gladden the hearts of many C2Coasters as it was such an amazing haven of good food, warmth and shelter.

Because of the strength of the wind, Ian decided to take the lower safer route and not to ascend Cringle End and cross Cringle and Cold Moors and the Wainstones as in such conditions Rachael could easily have been blown off her feet!

At first Rachael was a little grumpy because she had been looking forward so much to climbing on the spectacular Wainstones again but quickly accepted that this year it would be very dangerous.

Her awareness, knowledge and experience are growing all the time – she will become the most marvellous and responsible walker.

After a few words with Daddy, she realised that there would be a bonus – she would be able to come back for a special Christmas treat and stay with Ian at the Wainstones Hotel so she could play on the Wainstones and have lots of fun – she certainly sees the positive aspects and advantages of any situation!

As they approached Clay Bank Top by the beautiful path through the forest, it actually rained for about 15 minutes – their first rain on the C2C 3 as Rachael noted in her journal! Adding,

'And we had to walk two extra miles because our B&B is down at Chop Gate like last year!'

To Grosmont

Rachael and Ian actually stayed again at Forge House at Chop Gate with Robin and Jenny who gave them a lift up to Clay Bank Top next morning. This meant that Rachael's total mileage for the C2C 3 was 201 miles! Rachael had recorded in her journal just how much she enjoyed staying at Forge House.

'Robin and Jenny have lots of animals on their farm (smallholding). They have two cows, Doris and Nelly – Doris is pregnant with a calf – one baby bull called Gismo, four chickens, a few sheep and four lambs. One was born at the exact moment that we arrived there. I got to hold one of the lambs and watched Jenny bottle-feeding them. We are coming back in three weeks when Doris' calf is born. This place is fab!'

Rachael by now was so used to the next section of the C2C to Blakey Ridge that something spectacular would have had to happen to merit a mention in her journal. As it is all she said was – 'The walk over the moor to the Lion Inn is mostly flat – no phone boxes!'

In fact although the walk on the cinder bed of the old Ironstone railway is indeed fairly flat, the views are magnificent. That morning it was still very windy but reasonably warm and they could see for miles – as far east as the North Sea, over the endless undulating stretch of the Yorkshire moors and gentle, beautiful Rosedale. A sudden gust of wind blew Steph off her feet and deposited all the contents of her pockets on the path and in the heather. This made Rachael giggle as she scrambled around helping to gather up all the items and stuffed them back in Steph's pockets. 'The things that woman carries,' thought Ian!

At Blowarth Junction Rachael posed for several photos on the gate and then laughed and skipped her way ahead determined to catch at least one of the many baby grouse that were squeaking and scurrying in the heather. As previous years, she was completely unsuccessful but thoroughly enjoyed chasing them much to the annoyance of their loudly clucking mums!

With Rachael sprinting in front of Ian and Steph, racing the wind on the moor, it was not long before they reached The Lion Inn at Blakey Ridge, Rosedale.

Left: Helping out with a day-old lamb. **Right:** Making another friend at Forge House – Chop Gate.

Just when we thought the snow was over!

They had a very pleasant meal at the Lion Inn and an uneventful evening. This did not stop Rachael and Steph making everyone smile with their jokes and giggles – just two crazy kids together.

Steph left them next morning going by taxi to the nearest station where she caught a train back to Richmond. Apparently she had paid to leave her motorcycle in the backyard of 'a man with a carpet shop.' Strange place, thought Ian – but he had learned long ago not to look for any logic in Steph's actions.

Rachael noted in her journal – 'Steph left this morning and I met 'Fat Betty' again and someone had nicked my 20p. Then we walked to the Fryup monument and someone had nicked my 20p there too!'

Left: Rosedale. **Right:** Slow down, Rachael!

Left: Now where is that 20p I buried here last year! **Right:** The head of Fryup Dale and another 20p missing!

(Readers will remember that last year, with Catherine's secret help, Rachael had buried a coin at each monument to make sure that she had to return the next year to collect them.)

Actually while Rachael was searching the ground around 'Fat Betty', a couple who had been staying at the Lion Inn went past them and quickly disappeared into the distance. Shortly the gentleman stopped and apparently had spotted an adder but then the couple walked on rapidly down towards Glaisdale on the path called Cut Road.

At that point Rachael and Ian, as last year, were walking 'in a bubble of sunshine' whilst huge black rain clouds gathered on every side of them and soon it began to pour down but not on them! Does Ian have an agreement with the Almighty, I wonder?

Further down, the couple were getting soaked and stopped to put on all their rain gear – Rachael and Ian were completely dry. As you may imagine, Rachael thought that was really funny – 'Serves them right for passing us!'

They stopped at the Arncliffe Arms at Glaisdale for a drink but did not

The sun shines on the righteous?

realise that the 'speedy couple' had gone inside for lunch. While they were sitting outside chatting to yet another couple with two dogs, Rachael had a minor disaster – (the quote from her journal),

'Whoops! I had an accident. I tipped a whole glass of cola into Daddy's lap. He was very wet and cold because there was ice in it. I was sorry but I couldn't help laughing – he looked so shocked! Mac and Archie, their dogs, thought it was very funny too because they jumped up and down and barked.'

Before Rachael and Ian left, this lovely couple sponsored Rachael for £20 – she was ecstatic!

'Aren't I lucky, Daddy?' she exclaimed proudly.

Just before Egton Bridge, Rachael and Ian overtook the 'speedy couple' who had stopped for another snack so it was very happy and triumphant Rachael who reached Grosmont first – 'What an awesome competitor!' thought Ian.

Right on time, the steam train waiting in Grosmont Station greeted her with a loud whistle and a huge bellowing cloud of steam. Later Rachael and Ian met the 'speedy' couple again when they had a drink together sitting outside the Station Tavern and found that they were all staying at the same B&B.

At breakfast next morning, after hearing all about Rachael's amazing adventures, they gave Rachael the birthday card they had bought for her and sponsored her for another £20 – what a fantastic gesture! Rachael was absolutely thrilled.

In her journal is the entry, 'People are so kind to me – another £20 to help my school and our Mountain Rescue Team so that is £40 since we left the Lion Inn! And we didn't get wet and I saw two phone boxes. What a fab day! I love this C2C!'

Clever dogs around here!

The Last Day – Grosmont to Robin Hood's Bay

They set off in torrential rain – what a way to start your last C2C day and your ninth birthday as well! They went back down to Grosmont Station because Ian wanted to film Rachael there and record her feelings about her last day of the C2C 3. Because of the delay, the 'speedy couple' were far, far ahead up that dreadfully steep hill from Grosmont – the hill that all C2Coasters dislike with a passion.

'Come on, Daddy!' urged Rachael, 'We can beat them!' And she, actually, began to sprint up what she calls 'Huff & Puff Hill' in her determination to overtake them.

'Where does she get all that energy from?' thought a bemused Ian 'and particularly after all the terrible conditions she has overcome and her dreadful days of sickness when any ordinary person would have given up!' He was glowing with pride. Did she overtake them? Of course she did – just as the couple reached the top of Huff & Puff Hill before beginning to cross the moorland.

It wasn't long before it stopped raining so, unbelievably, they only had one hour and 15 minutes of rain on the whole of the 17 days of this C2C 3.

They walked on through Littlebeck and up the beautiful woods of Sneaton Forest to the Heritage Cave where, Rachael as always, posed for several photos. They stopped for refreshments at Falling Foss Tea Garden – that fabulous, tranquil little haven nestling at the top of the magnificent Falling Foss waterfall in a magical fairy glen. Originally it was built as a gamekeeper's cottage in the grounds of Midge Hall and in the 1900's had been a tea garden. However by the 1960's, it was abandoned and sadly became derelict.

Left: 'Dad, I think I must be growing!' **Right:** Rachael and Falling Foss Waterfall again.

In the 1980's Steph and Jack Newman fell in love with Midge Hall and its idyllic surroundings and bought it and renovated the wonderful, peaceful little tea garden opening it in July 1980. What better place could you find for a family where children can play, use their imagination to explore and build dens and even play 'pooh sticks' in the stream flowing under the footbridge – (pooh sticks provided!). There is even a climbing wall and wooden animals.

Rachael and Ian did not indulge in one of the sumptuous cream teas but did enjoy delicious ice creams. As you may imagine, Rachael did not spend long playing there as she had a goal to reach – Robin Hood's Bay!

They wound their way up through the enchanting woods and onto the open moorland in bright sunshine. Time for a quick snack so as she did the first year, Rachael climbed a tree there and sat perched in it eating her lunch – not far to go now. (Last year when they had walked with Catherine, Ian had taken a slightly different route.)

They carried on through High Hawsker and the caravan park and were soon on the last lap – the spectacular cliff path to Robin Hood's Bay. Rachael barely noticed the beautiful scenery before her or the white capped waves of the wind-driven North Sea far below. She was truly bursting with excitement!

She could hardly wait to finish. They paused frequently so that Ian could take photos – after all this was an historic event – the unbelievable achievement of his brave little daughter to be the youngest ever Triple Coast to Coaster!

Eventually they saw a little figure in the distance wearing a bright pink fleece – me – Grandma Joyce – I could hear Rachael shouting with delight high on the cliffs above me.

I had promised Rachael that I would come to Robin Hood's Bay to welcome her and meet her on the cliff path so we could all walk into Robin Hood's Bay together. She was ecstatic – so full of joy and triumph, she just glowed!

Left: A cream moustache. **Right:** This little girl just cannot pass an animal without saying 'Hello!'

Nearly there ...

We all struggled against the wind which was really strong – Ian held onto Rachael and I held on to whatever was around – fence posts, gates and walls! As we all looked across the North Sea to our first sight of Robin Hood's Bay, as always I was in tears – it is such an emotional moment for anyone who has walked all the way from the Irish Sea at St. Bees. Before long, we reached the gate that marks the end of the C2C path and the end of Rachael's amazing challenge – she had done it – overcome tremendous obstacles and won!

Left: ... and look at that big smile! **Right:** Still enough energy to RUN to the finish after three C2Cs!!!

It is hard to describe how she looked or indeed, how Ian and I felt – words are totally inadequate for such an occasion.

We all walked jubilantly to the top of the hill and there met her mum, Catherine and Rachael's elder sister, Emily, who had travelled up from London. They had all come to greet her and celebrate her fabulous success and her 9th birthday. They congratulated her and gave her huge hugs.

We walked down the steep hill to the beach with an elated Rachael, as always, running way ahead of us, arms raised, shouting with happiness – she was just incandescent with joy and pride!

Naturally, she was first on the now familiar beach and ran around excitedly, arms outstretched, jumping and splashing just like any ordinary little girl delighted to be on sand at the seaside – but as we know, this is no ordinary little girl!

The sea wasn't too far out and the waves blown by the wind kept rushing up the beach nearly soaking our feet. Eventually, Rachael gave us the pebbles that Ian had carried all the way from St. Bees – one for each of us and we all threw them into the North Sea and completed the tradition by 'officially' dipping our feet in the water.

Rachael tried her hardest to pull Daddy into the sea and actually managed to get his feet and the bottom of his trousers thoroughly wet. Lots of photos, hugs and congratulations and then, as is the custom, we climbed up to Wainwright's Bar so that Rachael could sign the register of the Coast to Coasters again.

Left: With 'Willy' and the scroll made by Catherine on the slip way at Robin Hood's Bay! **Right:** Come on, Dad – let's get our feet wet!

We had all brought birthday cards and presents for Rachael and Catherine had made her a fantastic poster congratulating Rachael on her success and was clearly very proud of her little sister – what a kind girl she is!

I had been to my local chocolate shop and they had made a unique chocolate champagne bottle for Rachael to celebrate her success. On it were the words –

9th BIRTHDAY

RACHAEL

'C2C 3'

17.4.2013

Rachael was overjoyed! Deservedly, she was completely the centre of attention – she just loved it and her face shone with happiness.

As she signed the register, the man behind the bar looking at all her presents said, 'Obviously, it's your birthday and you have just finished the C2C – how old are you?'

'I'm nine today', answered Rachael.

'Oh!' replied the man, somewhat smugly 'Then you are not the youngest child to walk the C2C – I've heard of a seven year old girl who walked it!'

Triumphantly, pointing at Rachael, I had the greatest pleasure informing him that the little miracle sitting in front of him **was** that seven year old and she had done the C2C **again** at the age of eight so now, at the age of nine, she was a triple Coast to Coaster and a Record Breaker!

Rachael celebrates her amazing triple C2C adventure ... what is next, we wonder!!!

'Oh, my God! Really! Congratulations!' he replied astonished and humbled.

We celebrated with a lovely meal and several drinks then climbed the steep hill from the beach to our B&B the very top of the hill – 'Thackwood' – a lovely welcoming place.

Rachael had always wanted to stay overnight at Robin Hood's Bay after completing the C2C but on each of the previous two walks, they had come straight home to Old Water View.

This time however, to celebrate Rachael's ninth birthday, she had her special treat – her overnight stay sharing a room with Daddy and Catherine slept with me. Bless her, Catherine was genuinely proud of her little sister and I'm really proud of her for being so understanding at the tender age of ten.

For readers who may be wondering who won the phone box challenge – well, I bet you can guess – Rachael, of course, by a huge margin! This was also the result of the Tractor Challenge in spite of Ian's repeated attempts at cheating – will he never learn?

Next day, we drove home to Old Water View in my little red car. After all the excitement and effort it is hard to 'come down to earth' but when you own a very busy restaurant with accommodation, you simply have 'to get back to work.'

Rachael was very happy to be home but was already planning what they could do next – so watch out, Ian, you have lots more challenging adventures to come with your amazing little walker and kindred spirit, Rachael!

Rachael's wandering boots

Readers will remember that Rachael left her boots behind at home on her C2C 2 and we had to drive back to Old Water View to retrieve them.

You may not be surprised to be told that Rachael also left her boots behind at Thackwood, Robin's Hood's Bay on her C2C 3. They were returned free of charge by Packhorse – ready for her next challenge.

Some thoughts on this fantastic C2C 3

I know that Ian will hate this part because he avoids the limelight and abhors praise no matter how deserved it may be – but I'm going to write it anyway!

Rachael's fabulous achievement was due to her cheerful and sometimes grim determination and unbelievable bravery and courage but also to the meticulous planning, wide knowledge, resourcefulness and loving care of her Daddy, Ian.

Readers, who like me, are walkers, climbers or trekkers will appreciate the immense value of an inspirational and experienced leader or guide such as Ian who will give you confidence to tackle seemingly impossible feats and motivate you to strive to succeed: someone who simply makes the difference between disaster and safety – failure and success! So well done, Ian – you are the best!

And now what do I say about our wonderful little walker, Rachael?

Yes! She completed her third Coast to Coast at 4pm on April 17th 2013 – her ninth birthday. This makes her a triple Coast to Coaster – three C2C walks within 20 months and so she is a remarkable Record Breaker too!

This C2C 3, mainly because of the dreadful weather, was very difficult for Rachael but she battled on tenaciously through snow and ice, high and bitterly cold winds, extra miles and sickness and won – an incredible triumph!

I remember vividly Rachael saying as she tried on my Everest down jacket for the first time,

'I know you went to Everest Base Camp, Grandma Joyce, but I am going to climb Everest!'

Everyone who reads her awe-inspiring story will never dare to doubt that if this continues to be Rachael's ambition, one day she will succeed!'

So congratulations, Rachael, you are a super star!

Writing my story of these three wonderful C2Cs has made me realise just how proud I am to be part of this remarkable family – Rachael, Catherine and Ian – you are all heroes.

At the point of finishing this book, the walks have raised approximately £5,000 to be shared between Patterdale C of E School and The Patterdale Mountain Rescue Team – well done everyone.

Rachael's 'Moment to Shine' with Dad's Olympic Torch

A nine-year-old girl is thought to be the youngest ever triple coast-to-coaster – stealing the limelight from her inspirational dad.

Rachel Moseley, from Patterdale, completed the 192-mile trek for the third time on her ninth birthday in April.

Her accomplishments mean that dad Ian's historic leg of the Olympic torch relay has already been overshadowed, barely a year after the event.

Ian, 53, who runs Old Water View guest house, says: "Rachael was the youngest person to complete the C2C in 2011, aged seven years, three months and 23 days.

"Her older sister Catherine then wanted to do it too, so Rachael did it again – making her the youngest person to do it twice in a year.

"She completed it for the third time in April on her ninth birthday. She is the world record holder for being the youngest triple coast-to-coaster."

News of Rachael's accomplishments emerged as Ian reflects on the 12 months since the torch relay came to Cumbria.

He was picked out of 100,000 nominees to be one of the 8,000 "heroes" who carried the flame around Britain.

London 2012 organisers had hoped to use the torch to capture the imagination of the public, to recognise the many deserving people in the UK and to build up the excitement ahead of the games.

The thousands of people who lined Cumbria's streets to catch a glimpse of the iconic torch were testament to its success.

More than 50 north and west Cumbrians were awarded the honour of carrying the flame.

Ian was nominated for his lifelong dedication to children, stemming from his first voluntary work aged 14 in a hospital, to his 16 years as a Samaritan volunteer.

Since then he has founded Millers

Who's the hero now? Ian Moseley, 53, from Patterdale, carried the Olympic Torch through Workington. Since then his daughter Rachael, nine, has become the world's youngest triple coast to coast walker
LOUISE PORTER

Homes for Children, which is dedicated to caring for vulnerable or abused children, and completed a number of fundraising challenges.

Ian carried the torch through Workington on June 21. He recalls: "It was a fantastic day, that will stay with me forever. It was my middle daughter Catherine's 10th birthday that day, and so she feels I did it for her.

"It was a truly magical day, but a one-off and life has to go on. Rachael's achievements have outshone mine."

Ian framed the uniform for protection and has stored the torch in a safe place, to be handed to Catherine, Rachael and 25-year-old daughter Emily in years to come.

However, photographs of him holding the torch are proudly on display in the guest house, and continue to spark admiration from his guests.

About the Author –
Joyce Buxton

I am a Derbyshire 'girl' – now happily retired to the Peak District.

I am a Rotarian being a proud member of the Rotary Club of Bakewell where I am Chairman of Youth Services and as such I am privileged to be able to help people locally, nationally and internationally. I am also International Ambassador of F.I.N.C.H. – (Friends International Network of Children's Homes) – founded by my friend and Rachael's dad, Ian Moseley. It is a network of like-minded people who care for vulnerable children all over the world. Working with Kathmandu Metro Rotary Club we support a village in the Himalayan foothills and orphanages in Nepal as well as many participating in numerous worldwide projects.

I am an ex-nurse and a retired teacher and have walked most of my life and trekked for many years in Nepal – Everest Circuit and Annapurna Base Camp, the Annapurna Circuit etc. and have completed many of the long distance walks in the UK including the Pennine Way, West Highland Way, Hadrian's Wall and the Coast to Coast twice – West to East and East to West. At the age of 76 on 1st October 2013, I am starting my third Coast to Coast walking on my own.

So as you can see we are a walking 'family' and very familiar with and love that wonderfully varied and beautiful walk that is the Coast to Coast.

I have written this book using the journals of Ian and Rachael and the endless long happy phone conversations with Ian – it has been a pleasure.

Joyce – The Annapurna Circuit, Nepal.